# Digging Deep

Fostering the Spirituality of Young Men

# Digging Deep

Fostering the Spirituality of Young Men

Michael J. Downey

Saint Mary's Press
Winona, Minnesota

Genuine recycled paper with 10% post-consumer waste.
Printed with soy-based ink. 50693

The publishing team included Janet Claussen, development editor; Alan DeNiro/Buuji, Inc., copy editor; Eric Vollen/Buuji, Inc., typesetter; Cären Yang, designer; Isaac Zafft, cover artist, Winona, MN; pre-press, printing and binding by the production services department of Saint Mary's Press.

The acknowledgments continue on page 110.

Printed in the United States of America

Printing: 9 8 7 6 5 4 3 2 1

Year: 2011 10 09 08 07 06 05 04 03

ISBN 0-88489-803-2

For John-Michael & Patrick,
two quite wonderful young men
and my daily source of delight;
and for Marian,
my very best friend.

# Contents

# Introduction

"The child grew and became strong, filled with wisdom; and the favor of God was upon him." (Luke 2:40)

## Tread Carefully

This book is like a map for use on a journey to unearth the sacred treasures of manhood. Exploring the inner world of the spiritual has the potential to be life-giving and richly rewarding. But this process requires digging; it is not to be undertaken lightly. A man's spirituality is a powerful thing. This journey should begin only if you are ready to engage in the process and be transformed. Jesus promised the reward of life to the full (John 10:10) to those who followed him.

## Sacred Circles

A priest working in Africa wondered why—after a century of his church building and operating schools, hospitals, and social programs—there were no Christians among the adults of the villages. One day he resolved to go and speak with one of the tribal elders:

> I asked Ndangoya if we could speak to him about something very important. He immediately sent for the elders of the three neighboring kraals, and when they arrived, he asked what I wanted to talk about. I said I wanted to talk to them about God, and he answered, "Who can refuse to talk about God?"
>
> I then pointed out that we were well known among the Masai for our work in schools and hospitals, and for our interest in the Masai and their cattle. But now I no longer wanted to talk about schools and hospitals, but about God in the life of the Masai, and about the message of Christianity. Indeed it was for this very work of explaining the message of Christianity to the different peoples of Africa that I came here from far away.
>
> Ndangoya looked at me for a long time, and then said in a puzzled way, "If this is why you came here, why did you wait so long to tell us about this?"
> (Vincent J. Donovan, *Christianity Rediscovered*, p. 22)

Is it possible that in many theology and religious education classes and youth groups, we spend so much time doing good things that we miss the opportunity to engage the message of Christianity through what it means to be, and live, as a man? What could be more wonderful than sitting in a circle of men, talking about God and the promises of Christianity in our lives?

Regardless of whether it was an African tribal council, a group of Native American braves, or King Arthur's legendary Knights of the Round Table, men have gathered in circles to address the sacred business of manhood. Rites of passage have in the past provided the opportunity for boys to take their place as men in these gatherings. Young males' participation in these rituals was of utmost importance and an undisputed sign of their attainment of manhood.

Today, it is up to fathers, teachers, priests, scout leaders, youth ministers, and mentors to provide opportunities for meaningful conversation with the next generation. The focus of this book is to help initiate and sustain circles of men to discuss, ponder, and pray together both in relationships with each other and God.

## Sacred Business

Although traditional wisdom tells us the conversations are still essential, the content of men's sacred business has undergone changes. In the past, people with power accepted inequalities as part of a natural order of things. As a result, systems of structural dominance were unjust but unquestioned. White people dominated people of color, men dominated women, and the rich dominated the poor. These inequities are in direct contradiction to the Gospels, which encourage all people to live in equality as sisters and brothers.

The system known as "patriarchal domination" or "male domination" resulted in psychological, spiritual, and physical violence. The most obvious victims of this power abuse were women and girls in society; the patriarchal system denied them most opportunities for advancement, and kept them from fulfilling the potential of their birthright. Although much has changed in the last thirty years to improve the status of women in society, there are still aspects of the culture that do not only harm females throughout the world, but also their male counterparts.

We will continue to miss the mark of genuine equality unless we address the liberation of males from the dominant patriarchal societal structures that prevent men from living lives to the full. Traditional stereotypes that limit boys from developing into the fullness of their potential manhood are no less violent than the outdated thinking that discourages girls from reaching their potential. Unjust systems of the past limited girls by restricting them in what they could "do." Those same systems *define* boys by what they "do" and restrict how males can "be" as men.

## Gender Differences

Although gender studies suggests that more females are naturally better at "being" and relating, and the majority of males are inclined toward "doing," stereotypes can limit the profound mystery that men and women are made in the image and likeness of

God. However, just as there are physiological differences that influence the development of males and females even before birth, it is also important to recognize psychological gender differences.

The psychologist Erik Erikson observed that the path to wholeness is different for men and women. Although the culture has reinforced certain masculine and feminine characteristics, both men and women need to develop a full range of skills and abilities to negotiate life with meaning. Another psychologist, Carl Jung, saw certain qualities as being "feminine" and "masculine," but he did not think that they were exclusively male or female. Rather, to be whole, one had to psychologically integrate both masculine and feminine qualities. Jung recognized a balanced or "whole person" by their integration of the whole range of human qualities. The psychological insights of both these psychologists show us that "stereotypes" of what a male or female should be are not only false, but inequitable for both men and women.

When we confine men to the world of doing, their inner life becomes impoverished. What many men find is that even if they wish to rein in their doing for the sake of their being, they lack the skills to do so. Many find that they have either forgotten how to attend to their spiritual lives effectively, or never learned how in the first place. As a result, their relationships with God and others are not as rich and life-giving as they could be. This leaves many men constantly yearning and searching for something more; something, ironically, which is as close as their own breath. As the Scriptures remind us, God "who gives life and breath to everything " (Acts 17:25).

## Spirituality and Wholeness

Our Catholic Tradition teaches that we are spiritual beings incarnated in a physical body for the duration of what we call our "life." People of many different religions have always believed that a person's spirit leaves their body when they die, so it seems to be a universal phenomenon that our spirituality is inseparable from our life. No spirit, no life. It is vital for "life" that we attend to our spiritual needs. Our spirituality is our life longing for wholeness. This is where we find meaning, and a man can only find meaning in life as a man. Essentially, wholeness (or holiness) is what we seek to satisfy our hungers, yearnings and longings in life. As St. Augustine said, "our hearts will not be at peace until they rest in You." There is simply no other way to find wholeness, peace, or happiness. Neither spiritual hunger nor restlessness will go away if ignored. It will surface in other, disguised forms for attention.

The role of religion is to address this restlessness toward God. Religion, at its best, helps men and women find and bind together their wholeness as they journey through life with all of its joys, delights, crises, struggles, and moments of ordinary, everyday living. Religion and spirituality are not mutually exclusive. Religion needs spirituality for vitality; spirituality needs religion to provide the wisdom of the ages.

Wise men of spirit, or spiritual men, make a difference for the better in their families, in their workplace, among their friends and in their world; they make good husbands and fathers. The clinical evidence indicates that they are happier, healthier, and they live longer.

## The Spiritual Life of Adolescent Males

When boys' needs are met in a nurturing environment, they will develop into men of spirit with the skills to develop a healthy inner life. Jesus urged his followers to "go into your room" in secrecy (Matt. 6:6). That "room" is the sacred domain of the inner life. Fostering the spiritual life of young men involves learning to be comfortable in that room, which is a place to be still, reflect, and communicate and trust in someone—or something—outside themselves.

The Gospel of John tells the story of two young men meeting Jesus for the first time (1:35–39). When Jesus asked them what they were looking for, it seems that they didn't know, or didn't know what to say, and so they just blurted out the first thing that came to mind: "where are you staying?" This tells us a lot about young males and their enthusiasm in seeking, as well as their difficulties in awareness and communication.

Girls on average are naturally better at communication than are boys. Some researchers say that emotional literacy is the most significant factor when considering the development of boys. However, in my experience of working with boys in high schools and retreat programs, I know that boys are most capable of developing healthy emotional and spiritual awareness, as well as good communication skills. What we need are the right conditions and the patience to have the conversations that need to take place.

## The Passage into Manhood

Masculinity is a gift, a pearl of great price. Manhood needs to be celebrated as essentially very good, but becoming a man is complex. In the past, particularly in traditional societies and cultures, the men would take the boys away into a secret or sacred place at the appropriate times to facilitate their growth or maturity to manhood. This was seen very much as a spiritual rite or sacred ritual. Individuals would leave as boys and return as men. The transition, or adolescence, lasted as long as the rite of passage. Rites of passage have largely disappeared from modern Western culture; the result is that adolescence can ambiguously span any length of time between ages eleven or twelve to the mid- to late-twenties.

Over the last few years, I have designed and facilitated a number of three-week retreats for young men, ages fourteen to sixteen. The group size has varied from twenty-five to fifty. The retreat involves service to the poor and marginalized, Scripture study, and silent reflection. At the beginning of the three weeks, the boys enjoy the satisfaction of "doing" something with, and for, the poor and marginalized. However, they find the other aspects of the retreat challenging. By the end of the three weeks, they also appreciate the nourishment of Scripture study and of the quiet reflection time. Having learned to dig deep, they are no longer boys, but men of faith. On each occasion I have been involved with this retreat, others have marveled at how we begin with boys and finish three weeks later with fine, young, emotionally articulate men of depth, maturity, and integrity.

# Overview of This Manual

*Digging Deep: Fostering the Spirituality of Young Men* is a resource manual with activities designed to take young men from the surface mode of "doing" to a deeper place where they can experience the treasure of "being." Part 1 places considerable emphasis on preparing the soil and developing competence with the tools for digging beyond the surface of conversations with adolescent males. Part 2 focuses on specific issues, including identity, power and anger, and sexuality. The appendix includes a father/son retreat designed for a weekend format, but this is easily adaptable to other time frames and venues. The appendix also contains suggestions for coordinating the activities in this book with parallel sessions for girls, found in Saint Mary's Press *Voices* series.

## Who Can Use This Manual

*Digging Deep: Fostering the Spirituality of Young Men* is for use by men working with adolescent males in an all-male environment. The material works best with males aged thirteen to nineteen, although junior high boys may benefit from some of the simpler activities, and most activities can be easily adapted for young adult men in their twenties.

Interestingly, my experience has been that it is often at the initiative of mothers that the spiritual quest of manhood often begins. My first attempt to have a retreat for fathers and sons resulted in widespread cancellations at the last minute. I received a steady stream of phone calls from mothers telling me that they wanted their husbands and sons to participate, but that their husbands, and sometimes their sons, had fears and apprehensions. (See p. 89 in chapter 4 of part 2 for a list of common fears and fallacies.) I was able to convince the mothers that these fears were unfounded, and I encouraged them to use their influence. They did and the fathers and sons agreed to go. The retreat and many more since have been successful, thanks to the initiative of these boys' mothers. They saw what was needed and provided the initial momentum.

## Praxis of the Sessions

Each section in *Digging Deep* begins with an overview presenting theological and spiritual background for the adult leader. In part 1, there are activities to practice skills such as listening and talking, telling stories, journaling, and different forms of prayer, including rituals. The activities in part 2 delve more deeply into specific topics, beginning with a focus activity or stimulus (such as a movie or story); then moving to written and verbal reflection by individuals through group discussion, journaling, and prayer. Again, the focus is less on "doing" than on learning to "be."

## How to Get Started

Begin with the sacred circle. Simply coming together in circles changes the immediate environment. Each time you gather boys into a circle for discussion or prayer, draw attention to the fact that all present are now included together in this circle of men. Acknowledge this every time so that it does not go unnoticed. The circle is a powerfully inclusive shape in which to gather for the following reasons:

- no one sits at the "head" and therefore the circle is a symbol of equality of power and prestige
- everyone in a circle is equally visible, so no one can go unnoticed
- a circle is a natural gathering shape, as demonstrated by the way boys will huddle in a circle on a sports field to discuss their game plan and motivate each other
- in a circle, the focus tends towards the center; whether this is something physical, like a candle; or something intangible, like an issue for discussion

### Creating the Environment

A few select items can transform a regular meeting space into sacred space. Decide with the group what is needed for your sacred space and where the items will be placed. Begin by asking the group members about "a man's sacred space." What does it look like? Suggest some simple ideas like a Bible and a candle; the group, however, may have other suggestions: pieces of wood, stones, posters, or a simple cross or crucifix. Encourage them to explain the symbolism or significance of each suggestion. Give responsibility for each item to a member of the group.

### Involving the Senses

As often as possible, enhance your meeting space and time with music, fire, and incense, involving as many of the five senses as possible. Keep charcoal briquettes in a clay or metal pot half-filled with sand as a convenient and contained way to build a fire outside. Small pieces of incense, added to the fire, contribute to the mood of prayer, signifying something important. Recall that since ancient times, incense has been a sign of holiness and purification; as part of our sacred rituals it communicates awe and respect for God. It also symbolizes our prayers rising to God as the incense smoke rises to the skies or heavens above.

It is also a good idea to keep a collection of music that sets the tone for prayer and ritual. The music selections below are representative of a good "male sound." They are subtle and gentle, and the voices are obviously men's voices. Using these helps dispel the falsehood that religious music might not be "masculine":

- Chesnokov, Pavel, "We Praise Thee," St. Petersburg Chamber Choir, Nikolai Korniev, conductor from *Credo,* Phillips 446 089-2.
- *Sacred Treasures: Choral Masterworks from Russia* (1998). San Francisco: Hearts of Space, 11109-2.
- *Sacred Treasures II: Allegri's Miserere* (1999). Osnabruk Youth Choir, conductor Johannes Rae. San Francisco: Hearts of Space, 11112-2.

### Tips for Success

- Model what you wish for them to become. Boys need men to show them they way.
- Be yourself. Don't pretend.
- Make sure you have thoroughly read through the activities you have chosen beforehand. Know where you are going with these. Make sure you have all the materials and resources you need.
- Be flexible and adaptable. Adapt these activities to the boys you work with. Do not attempt to adapt the boys to the activities.
- Be prepared for things to work out differently from what you expect.
- Communicate your expectations and wishes frequently and clearly.
- Be open to suggestions and say so.
- Make your young men welcome and responsible for welcoming each other.
- Trust in the divine loving Providence (and divine sense of humor) that brought this group together.
- Pray.

## Resources

### Male Spirituality

Pable, Martin. *The Quest for the Male Soul: In Search of Something More.* Notre Dame, IN: Ave Maria Press, 1996. Pable, a Capuchin friar draws on his experience in retreat work and psychology to give an easily accessible and clear picture of what male spirituality is all about.

Pryce, Mark. *Finding a Voice: Men, Women, and the Community of the Church.* London: SCM Press, 1996. With an understanding that we are the Church, Pryce gives insights into the world of male spirituality and its significance to men and their relationships.

Rohr, Richard. *Quest for the Grail.* New York: Crossroad Publishing, 2001.

Rohr, Richard, and Martos, Joseph. *The Wild Man's Journey: Reflections on Male Spirituality.* Cincinnati: St. Anthony Messenger Press, 1992. In both these books, Rohr, a well-known Franciscan writer and speaker, uses myth blended with everyday men's experiences. In doing so he makes significant contributions to an understanding of masculine spirituality.

Sanford, John A. *The Man Who Wrestled with God: Light from the Old Testament on the Psychology of Individuation.* Rev. ed. New York: Paulist Press (1987). This is a most significant work of scholarship, but at the same time it is a good read. Sanford uses the psychology of individuation to make the wisdom of the Scriptures alive and relevant to the life of every man. This book remains ever fresh and full of wisdom.

## Male Psychology

Biddulph, Steve. *Manhood: A Book About Setting Men Free.* Sydney, Australia: Finch Publishing, 1994. Biddulph writes in everyday language about the most complex aspects of men's lives, and delivers much clarity. A good book for fathers and sons to read together.

Clare, Anthony. *On Men: Masculinity in Crisis.* London: Arrow Books, 2001. A most engaging and readable book, enlightening the search for what it means to be a man today. The book reminds the reader that the word "crisis" means both problem and opportunity.

Corneau, Guy. *Absent Fathers, Lost Sons: The Search for Masculine Identity.* Boston: Shambala Publications, 1991. Corneau has much wisdom on the father/son relationship and its consequences for the lives we live. This book reveals a great deal about the emotional and spiritual lives of men with its unique insights.

Kindlon, Dan, and Thompson, Michael. *Raising Cain: Protecting the Emotional Life of Boys.* New York: Ballantine, 1999. Coming from their experience working with boys as psychologists, this book gives a very recognizable glimpse into the inner life of boys.

Moore, Robert, and Gillette, Douglas. *King, Warrior, Magician, Lover: Rediscovering the Archetypes of the Mature Masculine.* San Francisco: HarperSanFrancisco, 1990. Using the four archetypes of the title, the authors offer a guide to self-transformation on the premises that men are complex and that there is no one "right" way to be a man.

Pollack, William S. *Real Boys: Rescuing Our Sons from the Myths of Boyhood.* New York: Random House, 1998. This is a foundational book about the psychology of boys and adolescents from the perspective of a psychologist.

Real, Terrance. *I Don't Want to Talk About It: Overcoming the Secret Legacy of Male Depression.* New York: Scribner, 1997. Perhaps one of the most valuable contributions to articulating and understanding the life of a male in our time and place. Real's insights reveal great wisdom and understanding. This book should be required reading before parenthood.

Tacey, David J. *Remaking Men: Jung, Spirituality and Social Change.* London: Routledge, 1997. Tacey's application of Jung's psychology to spirituality in a time of social change reflects on the nature of masculinity with insight and hope.

Thompson, Keith, ed. *To Be A Man: In Search of the Deep Masculine.* New York: Tarcher/Putnam, 1991. A collection of essays and interviews on a wide range of topics central to the lives of men, from an extensive range of poets and writers who all have some gold worth digging for.

**Part One**

# Tools for Digging

Before any dig begins, it is important to learn how to use the proper tools and equipment. Part 1 of this manual will introduce basic methods for loosening the layers of boys' inner lives. As men journey with boys in exploring spirituality, they will need to become comfortable with these *processes* so that they can foster spiritual development of young males. Each section in part 1 will provide the rationale for specific skills and activities that use these processes. These sections are a good place to begin as you form all-male groups in your school, parish, or community. As you become more comfortable using the skills, you will want to return to these tried and true methods to dig deeper. These can stand alone or become incorporated into other sessions. With good role modeling, boys will soon learn the tools of digging deeper into their own souls.

When implementing the activities in part 1, it is essential to establish the parameters of the zone by creating an atmosphere of trust from the very beginning. Begin gently and be aware that defenses will come down slowly but surely, as adolescent boys find that they can trust and count on one another. Remember, the main motivation of the adolescent is to *avoid embarrassment*. As boys find that they can trust their leader and one another, they will be more likely to risk venturing into the unknown or unfamiliar.

# Talking and Listening

## Overview

Getting boys to talk can be a challenge. There are many times when boys need and want to talk, but they may not give that impression. Sometimes a conversation will be dominated by a couple of individuals who tend to have a lot to say. As a result, others will sit there quietly and say nothing, possibly feeling like they have nothing to contribute. They might even feel locked out of the conversation. Get to know your group and be mindful of each boy present. Keep a mental note of who has spoken and who has not. The practices in this section are simple strategies can be used to give everyone the opportunity to speak.

The role of the adult leader, teacher, or facilitator is crucial in getting boys to talk and listen. An older male who can remember and reflect on his own adolescence can meet boys where they are emotionally and spiritually. To indicate openness and authenticity with boys, use phrases such as these:

- I remember being self-conscious about this . . .
- I didn't realize at the time that I was not the only one who felt like this . . .
- Sometimes, I am unsure about . . .
- I find it hard to say what I feel about . . .

Admitting your own discomfort can encourage conversations about topics from the mundane to the sacred. However, don't be tempted to go too deep too soon. Like all things that grow, building community takes time. Be patient. Remember also that there are times when boys need not talk. The wisdom of knowing when to persist in getting a boy to talk, and when to let them be silent, comes with experience.

Boys need to know they have been heard, but they also need to listen to adults and to each other. When working with groups of boys, especially when addressing sensitive or personal issues, remember that their main motivation is to avoid embarrassment at all times. It is not unusual for boys to interrupt, speak out of turn or over someone else, or "undercut" a peer with a funny or sarcastic comment. These defense mechanisms are an obstacle to learning to trust others and to sharing matters of great importance with each other. It is important to establish and be consistent with the ground rules of group conversation. Keep it simple:

- One person speaks at a time.
- If one person speaks, the rest will listen.

This pattern needs to be well established with boys before a conversation can begin. Conversation with boys requires developing the discipline of listening so that others will speak, and speaking so that others will listen. It is too easy to underestimate the significance of this simple but foundational principle. Again, time spent on creating the right environment is an invaluable investment.

### Talking and Listening Practice

#### Activity: The Talking Ball

Use a large ball to focus and ritualize speaking and listening within a group of boys. A basketball is one of the easiest of balls to catch, decreasing the chance of embarrassment. It is not as small as a baseball and not as slippery as the oval shape of a football.

This activity can be useful as an icebreaker to begin a session. Consider using this activity initially so that the boys become familiar and comfortable with the routine of talking and listening. Once the routine is established, this activity is helpful in introducing a new issue for consideration or for returning to issues that need reinforcement.

1. Gather boys in a circle, either standing or seated. Give these simple instructions:
   - This is a "Talking Ball." Only the person holding the ball is able to speak. If anyone speaks without holding the ball, then the ball cannot be passed to him next or within 5 minutes. As group leader, I will decide who gets passed the ball (As leader, you can make sure no one is left out and also that quieter boys get to speak. Once the procedure is established, you may choose to pass the ball to one of the boys to lead the conversation.) I will direct a question to the boy with the ball. Once he catches the ball, he has three options:
     - He simply answers the question;
     - He can ask a clarifying question; e.g., "When you say . . .", "Do you mean . . .", or "What exactly do you mean by . . .";
     - He may say "pass" and not answer the question. (If a number of boys choose to pass on a question or topic, this may be a cue that something needs to be addressed by the group at this or a later session.)
   After one of these three things happens, he passes the ball back to the leader.

2. Begin the process of slowly, tossing the ball easily to individuals, asking short, nonthreatening questions like:
   - What did you do during the week (weekend)?
   - What was the last movie you saw?
   - What was the last CD you bought?
     Work up to more involving questions gradually:
   - Do you think the government is doing enough about social justice issues (e.g., child poverty, the environment)?

You can then move to statements beginning in the following ways:

- One of the things that really makes me angry is when . . .
- What was sad from my primary school years was . . .
- I am happiest when . . .
- I think I was put on this earth because . . .

It may take several sessions to work up to the deeper questions, depending on the group dynamics. It is essential to practice the procedure of one person speaking and everyone listening. After a while you may not need the Talking Ball. If you want your group to address some serious issues and you have a good dynamic going, reintroducing the Talking Ball may be a good way of cueing the group into serious conversation.

### Alternative Activities

Gather boys into a circle. Use any one of the following techniques to encourage speaking and listening:

- Give turns for speaking according to color clothing; for example, those wearing something blue, then those wearing something white, and so on.
- Invite the boys to respond in a sequence depending on what season they were born in (moving from summer, winter, autumn, and spring). Then change the order.
- Randomly allocate boys into groups of four. Seek four responses to four questions.
- Number off one to three. Group the "ones" together then repeat the process with the "twos" and "threes." In response to a question or issue, ask the "ones" to say why people might feel very positive toward the issue, the "twos" to say why people might feel very negative toward the issue, and the "threes" to say why people might feel neutral toward the issue.
- Assign partners, or let the boys choose a partner. Get each to find out what his partner thinks about something, then ask them to reply on behalf of each other.
- Organize boys in groups of four to six. Each time you gather give a different boy the job of making sure that each boy in his group has spoken.
- Give each group a deck of cards or set of dice. Have them pick a card or roll the dice to determine the order of speaking.

# Telling Our Stories

## Overview

Since the beginning of time, men have gathered in a circle and told their stories. Stories bring to life the mythic past, ancient ancestors, and family and community history. They also help us come to know who we are as individuals and as a group. Wise elders would recall a mythic story from the past in response to what was happening at that moment because mythic stories have a timeless truth to them. The great mythic stories may or may not have ever really happened, but they are always true in a larger and deeper sense. We need to ponder the truth they contain because the stories themselves are often symbolic.

Beyond the mythic stories, we are often unaware of the theology in our own stories. Every time we see life coming out of our heartache and brokenness, we get an insight into the central Christian mystery of the Resurrection that came after Jesus' suffering and Crucifixion. All of us have had experiences that felt like a "crucifixion," or that we suffered our own "agony in the garden." We often use the phrase that someone has been given "a heavy cross to carry." Even if we do not realize it at the time, each time we use such an expression we touch on the Christian mystery of the Incarnation.

As St. Paul put it, "creation waits with eager longing for the revealing of the children of God" (Rom. 8:19). As young males become proficient at talking and listening, they will be ready to tell their own stories and listen to those of others. Most boys journey through adolescence without talking about their personal story at any depth; to do so would make them feel vulnerable and awkward. By not telling or hearing these stories, they often think that no one else feels like they feel. As a result they often feel alone. Boys who are lonely either are acutely aware of their loneliness, or they act out in a pretense that denies their loneliness. By the time boys reach adolescence, they get pretty good at pretending.

A good starting place for developing authenticity is getting young men in touch with their own life stories. When boys share their life stories they overcome loneliness. This overcoming of isolation addresses one of the very first aspects of spirituality mentioned in the Bible, that "it is not good that the man should be alone" (Gen. 2:18).

Each person's story is sacred. Once the group members have written their life stories in one meeting or session, the stories can be shared at group level over a number of meetings. This prevents "overload" and creates an environment where each story is reverenced as special, giving individuals the opportunity to revisit and develop their own stories.

## Practice in Telling Our Stories

### Activity: Writing and Telling My Story

As an adult leader, first prepare your own life story, using the directions in the following activity. A lot depends on the adult who models the activity. Many people think that his story is not spectacular enough. A story does not need to be spectacular—it only needs to be real. Words genuinely spoken from the heart always speak to the heart of another. Trust in the uniqueness of the gift that you are to the boys with whom you are present at this time.

Second, you will also need to write out the prompting questions with a large marking pen, one per sheet of newsprint to place on the wall when students write their life story. Here's a step-by-step explanation:

**1.** Still the group with a short centering meditation (see activity for centering in the section, "Reflection, Contemplation, and Meditation").

**2.** An adult leading the activity needs to tell his own life journey. This has to be genuine while obviously tempered with good judgment. Ideally, it should include at least one example of a struggle for wholeness during a time of brokenness. How did a difficult time turn out to be an opportunity for growth?

**3.** Make sure each person has his journal and a pen. Play some gentle relaxation music softly. (The purpose of the music is simply to "fill the space" between individuals in the room. It helps in removing distractions from movements and noises from within and outside the room. It helps give privacy as individuals focus on their task.)

**4.** Instruct the group on being focused and present to what they are about to do. Then slowly and deliberately give these instructions:
- Begin in the top left hand corner of a double page and write the time, date, and your place of birth.
- Go to the bottom right-hand corner of that double page and write today's date.
- Between these two points we are going to construct a road; or if your prefer, a river.
- What are the main turning points in your life? (Read these questions out slowly. Once group has begun the task, post these questions on the walls so that the boys can look at them for prompting.)
  - Birth of siblings?
  - Beginning school?
  - Beginning high school?

- Moved from house, towns, state?
- Happiest memories?
- Saddest memories?
- When did someone encourage you?
- When did someone disappoint you?
- Who were your best friends along your journey?
- When did someone make you feel special?
- When have you felt loved?

**Note:** This activity can be slow to start. Once they are "on a roll," this activity can easily take an hour or two. It may need to be finished at home before the next meeting. Follow up with the next activity, "Listening to Others' Stories."

### Listening to Others' Stories

Over a period of several meetings, or sessions in a retreat, ask for volunteers to share their stories with the group. One or two stories each gathering will build community and trust. This will encourage shy members of the group to tell their stories at later gatherings. However, sharing of one's story must be "challenge by choice." Individuals should not feel compelled to share their story if they do not wish to do so. They may elect to leave out details that they want to remain confidential.

Remind the group that the words "secret" and "sacred" come from the same source. We respect others by respecting the sacredness of their stories. Because of this, we do not break confidentiality by repeating their story outside the group.

**1.** Whenever the occasion arrives for a participant to share his story, begin by reminding the group to consciously practice listening.

**2.** When a person has shared their story, the group needs to remain silent for a short period (between 30 seconds and 1 minute). After this time, members of the group can make a comment of affirmation, support, or encouragement. They cannot make a judgment, give advice, or discuss aspects of the story. The task of the listener is to receive the story as a sacred gift. If this is done, the only response to someone's story is showing gratitude for that gift.

**3.** Consider designing a small ritual at the end of each story sharing. Members from the group may express gratitude for hearing the story by lighting a small candle.

# Journaling

## Overview

Many authors who write about boys' issues recognize that boys are generally less articulate than girls are. Often when asked what they think, an adolescent male might respond, "I don't know." Journaling is a good way of developing awareness, articulating thoughts in privacy, exploring ideas, and questioning. It develops both written and verbal expression. Some of the greatest writing of all time is the result of men's journals. Some examples are *Journal of a Soul* by Pope John XXIII, *Letters and Papers from Prison* by Dietrich Bonhoeffer, and *The Confessions of St. Augustine*. Even the classic television series *Star Trek* begins or ends each episode with a journal entry by the captain with the words "Captain's log, Stardate . . .".

It may seem surprising to some (but not to those who work with adolescent males), but the majority of young men are often unaware of how they feel and what they think. Those of us who have survived male adolescence must never forget not to overlook the obvious. Regularly stopping to raise thoughts and feelings regarding awareness gives young men the opportunity to develop the skills of self-reflection and also affirms the validity of what they feel and think. Their thoughts and feelings become integrated with, rather than estranged from, their selves. For this reason, it is not always necessary to go further and probe the reasons or seek explanations for their thoughts and feelings. Simply raising them to awareness is enough.

Experience working with boys indicates that if they receive encouragement to write a response or reaction to something, they then have something to say if asked later. Reading what they have written is less threatening than speaking unaided. If a boy doesn't know what he thinks, then a good starting place might be something like, "Most people seem to think . . . because they. . .". With regular practice, boys will become proficient and comfortable at journaling.

Each of the group members needs to have their own personal journal. Use a standard lined notebook; an unlined sketchpad may be better for other forms of expression, including poetry and art. Consider having the boys create their own journal.

## Code of the Journal

It is important to convey the message that the contents of a person's journal are privileged information. Once boys can see that they are in a safe environment where their privacy is respected, they develop the trust to try different ways of expressing themselves. Introduce and periodically review the following points about journaling:

- No one can read another person's journal unless the owner of that journal specifically invites them to do so.

   **Note:** Adults need to be careful in modeling this respect for privacy. In a classroom situation, in which material needs to be completed for assessment, two options are:

    - The student can show the teacher the journal has been completed by leafing through the pages without the teacher reading the journal;
    - The teacher can contract to maintain confidentiality with each class member not revealing his journal responses to others.

- When it comes to group discussion and sharing time, no one should feel compelled to share everything that is in his journal. Sharing is always "challenge by choice" and should never leave group members uncomfortable. "Challenge by choice" is a term often used with adventure–oriented activities. It is good to stretch out of our comfort zones and challenge ourselves by taking risks. In the process of overcoming our fears, we stretch ourselves and grow as individuals. When one confronts fears, it isn't the same as being traumatized by them. "Challenge by choice" allows each and every participant to choose the level at which he participates. Over time as trust in the leader and other group members increases, individuals will feel free to stretch their comfort zones and take risks, as they learn to trust the safety of their environment.

- When journaling, it is important to pay attention to all thoughts and feelings. Often boys will "self-censor" their thoughts, assuming that they are not religious enough. There is also the widespread misconception that personal reflection is somehow feminine and therefore not masculine. Writing down all thoughts and responses increases the possibility of discovering the sacred in the midst of the experience of everyday life.

## Journaling as a Springboard for Discussion

Mindful that many boys initially find communication of nonconcrete matters difficult, many journal exercises in this manual provide a number of questions for response. Each boy does not have to always respond to every question or point. On some occasions, a boy might find that he can respond to each and every point. On other occasions, he may find that he has a response to only one point. The points or questions to which a boy does not respond may provide "a point of return" to which he can come back to after he has heard what the others in the group have had to say.

# Journaling Practice

## Activity: Journaling as a Check-in

This exercise is useful at the beginning and end of a gathering, or as a focus during exploration of an issue that needs attention. Note that this is an awareness-raising exercise and not a therapy session. Its purpose is for young men to raise to their awareness how they feel and think about a particular issue, or at a particular moment.

The first time the group does this exercise, use the following explanation of the time length they will have to write:

> As a rule of thumb, three minutes is a good length of time. Three minutes is about the average length of expected concentration for the average adolescent male. In prime-time, commercial television advertisements are played as often as every three minutes. Many popular songs are three minutes long. Three minutes is the average waiting time in a line before people start getting restless and irritable. If someone is angry, a three-minute "time out" is often long enough to calm down. If a boy has little or no response to a particular issue, three minutes is not too long to wait until the rest of the group finishes, but this period of stillness is enough time to allow the mind and the body time to begin to settle. Three minutes is also an appropriate length of time for reflection and silence, unless otherwise noted.

(**Note:** Establish the three-minute discipline initially, extending it gradually for deeper reflection exercises that naturally take longer to process.)

**1.** Begin the activity by quoting Genesis: "[T]he Lord God called to the man, and said to him, 'Where are you?'" (Genesis 3:9)

**2.** In response, boys should take about three minutes to write their answer to one or more of these questions:

- How do I feel? Positive, negative, curious, disinterested?
- What do I need to say at this point?
- Is my attention here or somewhere else?
- Where am I at, at this moment? What "zone" am I in at this moment?
- Where/when was I aware/unaware of God looking for me today?

# Praying

## Overview

Praying takes many forms. Prayer is personal. Prayer can be communal. There is a difference between saying prayers and praying. To learn to pray, boys need men to model praying. When boys see a man pray they will want to be able to do the same. "He was praying in a certain place, and after he had finished, one of his disciples said to him, 'Lord, teach us to pray, as John taught his disciples'" (Luke 11:1). For a boy, "teach us to pray" means, "show me what to do," not "tell me what to say." Most of all, prayer is communication. A basic principle of communication skills is "If you think communication is about talking, you haven't been listening." To engage the group in a discussion about prayer, use the talking ball or some other method to elicit answers to the following questions:

- What is prayer?
- What are different forms of prayer?
- Is there a difference between saying prayers and praying?
- How do different religions/traditions pray?
- Muslims pray five times a day. How often do we pray?
- Name some prayer postures or physical expressions of prayer.

### Saying Prayers

Make copies of Handout 1-A, "Coming to God in Prayer." Instruct the boys to paste these prayers into their journals. The suggested prayers provide structure and form. It is a good concrete fallback and it provides a fixed focus for times of prayer, especially in the beginning of a group's life. Although other prayers can be introduced regularly, returning to the prayer sheet provides consistency, builds tradition within the group, and links the group into the living tradition of the Church.

### Prayer Practice

#### Activity: "Teacher, Teach Us to Pray"

This prayer practice focuses on the Lord's Prayer. It can stand alone or be used at the beginning and ending of a gathering time or other activity. As this is the prayer

Jesus left his followers, most Christians can recite it from memory. Unfortunately, because we are most familiar with it, we mistakenly think that we know it well. Visiting and revisiting this prayer with deliberate mindfulness will help discover this treasure again.

**1.** At the beginning of a gathering, sit in a circle around a lighted candle.

**2.** Ask someone from the group to read the passage from the Gospel of Matthew (6:9–15) where Jesus instructs his followers how to pray.

**3.** After the reading, be still for about one minute.

**4.** Have a second person from the group read the same passage again.

**5.** At the end of the gathering, repeat the same process previously described, using the parallel passage from the Gospel of Luke (11:2–4).

**6.** Close by explaining to the group, in your own words, that:

⚴ The Lord's Prayer is something that is familiar to all Christians. However, because we are familiar with it, we can take it for granted and not say it as mindfully as we possibly should. Reading it from the Scriptures can make us mindful of the slight variations in wording of this prayer, which in turn focus our minds on what we are saying.

## Activity: Using the Bible to Pray

Sometimes, the language and expressions of the Bible can seem a bit disconnected from the world of today. Praying with the Bible invites us to take more time to ponder what it might be saying to us. Wisdom-seekers have often used the Bible for prayer, a bit like the way an explorer uses a compass. When navigating the inner world of the spiritual, the ancient maps of the Bible are our best guides. Don't forget that, even with the best maps, many things at first may seem strange or different when exploring the unknown. That is the beauty of exploring where no one else has been. You get to experience a unique journey.

One interesting place in the Bible to explore is the Book of Proverbs. Some Scripture scholars think the Proverbs are the advice of a father to his son and possibly authored by King Solomon. Each time an issue surfaces within the group for attention, search the Book of Proverbs for what it has to say. Proverbs deals with issues like loyalty and faithfulness (3:3), cheating (11:1), pride (16:18), drinking too much (20:1), and the way to wisdom (10:11).

Another book to explore with boys is a passage from Daniel, referred to as "the song of three young men" (3:52–90). This passage can provide a focus for prayer over a number of weeks, highlighting a few lines each time.

The Psalms have been used for daily prayer since ancient times. They were probably originally songs. Unlike modern songs, the words in the psalms usually don't rhyme, but the thoughts in the psalms "rhyme." In a modern song, the words rhyme and so alternate lines might end with words like "love" and "dove," or "pain" and "rain." When thoughts rhyme, we almost have an echo effect using different words. For example, Psalm 1 begins: "Happy are those who do not follow the advice of the wicked," and then echoes this on the next line with the words "or take the path that sinners tread." Not following the advice of the wicked and not treading a sinner's path "sounds" like a rhyming thought. Another example is in Psalm 8 that begins, "Our Lord, our Sovereign, how majestic is your name in all the earth," and then echoes the thought with "You have set your glory above the heavens." Again the thought of the psalmist sounds similar.

The writers of the Psalms said some beautiful things and they also said some terrible things, wishing the worst on others. The Psalms give a snapshot of the best and the worst of human nature. Their ancient language can sometimes lead us to think that this was the case only with the ancients. If we are honest with ourselves, it is the case with us as well. We get angry, intolerant, and often think the worst of things and people. Usually, we repress and deny these reactions and feelings because we know they are "not nice" and we try to be good. Being open and honest before God, who loves us exactly how we are, is the first step in being open to God's transforming love, where even the worst of our inclinations and thoughts can be touched with grace and redeemed.

Read the Psalms slowly and repeatedly and let them paint a picture, related to the circumstances of daily life. For example:
- Feeling like everyone is against you? Read Psalm 3.
- Appreciate the wonder of creation? Read Psalm 8.
- Need to feel reassurance? Read Psalm 17.
- Feel grateful for your blessings? Read Psalm 21.
- Need help? Read Psalm 28.
- Need patience? Read Psalm 37.
- Wanting forgiveness? Read Psalm 51.

The Psalms address every aspect of daily life. Open them at random and see if they speak to you, or systematically start at Psalm 1 and read one psalm each day.

### Activity: Praying with Psalm 46:10

**1.** Gather the boys in a circle. Light a candle and place at the center of the group.

**2.** Read this passage of Psalm 46 as follows, saying each phrase slowly and deliberately. Take a breath between each phrase letting the silence fill the space between the words:

"Be Still and Know that I Am God!"
"Be Still and Know that I Am"
"Be Still and Know that I"
"Be Still and Know that"
"Be Still and Know"
"Be Still and"
"Be Still"
"Be"

**3.** Pause in silence for one minute.

**4.** Resume slowly and deliberately as before, taking a breath between each line as you say:

"Be"

"Be Still"

"Be Still and"

"Be Still and Know"

"Be Still and Know that"

"Be Still and Know that I"

"Be Still and Know that I Am"

"Be Still and Know that I Am God" (Psalm 46:10)

**5.** Pause in silence for one minute.

**6.** In your own words, tell the boys the following:

෴ Psalm 46 reminds us that sometimes we do not have to say anything in prayer. Just being still for a few moments unclutters our mind enough for God to enter our consciousness.

**7.** After this exercise, invite the boys to journal about what they experienced, or what became known to them in the moments of stillness. Give them brief instructions about writing down their thoughts, feelings, and responses. Suggest that they include one or more of the following:

- Thoughts: a memory of a person, conversation, event may have "popped" into one's mind, etc.
- Feelings: a moment of peacefulness, anxiety, restlessness, etc.
- Responses: gratitude for something or someone, desire to be faithful, longing for acceptance, etc.

**8.** Invite the boys to write in their journals the words of Psalm 46:10 as the words were spoken, beginning with the whole phrase: "Be Still and know that I am God." On the next line write: "Be still and know that I am," and so on, leaving off the last word with each subsequent line until the eighth line has only the word "Be." Then repeat the process in the reverse order adding one word with each subsequent line until they write the entire line "Be still and know that I am God."

### Activity: Journaling as Prayer

After journaling has become a natural part of the group process along with prayer, consider with the group that journaling is itself a form of prayer. Journaling, like other forms of prayer, is our response to God. Use the following step-by-step activity to engage boys in journaling as prayer:

**1.** Read aloud this verse from the Gospel of Matthew:

"Ask, and it will be given to you; search, and you will find; knock, and the door will be opened for you" (7:7).

**2.** Review your journal and identify "moments" of prayer for yourself by reflecting on these questions:

- What have you asked for?
- What have you been given?
- What have you been looking for?
- What have you found?
- What has been opened for you?

**3.** Use a different color pen or create symbols, like arrows or asterisks to identify:

- a moment when you felt good about what you wrote
- a moment when you were surprised by what you wrote
- a moment when you thought you had nothing to write and you wound up writing anyway

**4.** Invite the participants to think about the question, "What awareness do you have from moments spent journaling?"

**5.** Encourage the boys to take some of the moments they identified, and write a prayer using ordinary language. For example:

Lord, I felt good when I saw that my friends were waiting for me. Was that you letting me know of your presence?

# Reflection, Contemplation, and Meditation

## Overview

Meditation, contemplation, and reflection are ways of enhancing a person's prayer life. They help us bring our selves and our lives to God. An added benefit is that these techniques also calm the body and the mind. In a world where constant over-busyness continually stresses people, regularly using these practices is refreshing to the body, mind, and spirit.

The terms reflection, contemplation, and meditation are often used interchangeably. Instead, distinguish between them as follows:

- Reflection means to "think back" or to make a visible image of something. If we think back over something, that is reflecting. It raises to consciousness who and what passed through our day, week, or year. Socrates said that "an unreflected life was not worth living."

- Contemplation is the ability to focus on something now. Contemplation would be the response to God's question, "Where are you?" (Gen. 3:9). In our busy world, contemplation helps us not to let life slip us by. When we are contemplative, we are present to particular moments, and we notice things that we might otherwise not notice. This sort of single-minded focus requires more effort than one might think. When one begins to contemplate something, we soon notice how our minds are easily distracted.

- Meditation enables us to become truly receptive. To meditate, we simply empty our minds and try not to think of anything. It is not that we focus on nothing so much as we focus on no thing. The ancient Greeks used the word "kenosis," which means emptying. This form of meditation is an emptying of the mind without focus on any "thing" or phrase. By emptying our minds, we become more receptive, creating space for God to enter. This is why Psalm 46 advises us to "be still" so that we can "know." It is one of those cases where paradoxically, less is more. An example of meditation, particularly in Arthurian literature, is "The Knight's Vigil." The night before starting on a quest, a knight would sit in the chapel or in a sacred space outdoors all night and keep a silent vigil, remaining open to God's will for him and his quest.

## Practicing Reflection, Contemplation, and Meditation

### Activity: Centering Exercise

Each time young men gather to reflect, meditate, contemplate, ponder, reflect, listen, or pray, it is necessary for them to center themselves. This is a simple process of slowing down and refocusing in order to become present to what one is doing. It is a process of turning our attention away from the myriad distractions and influences that clutter our minds so that we can be mindful of our actions. This is also an effective mechanism for stress reduction. The time length of the practices can be adjusted by gradually lengthening the periods of silence. As a leader, you are there to introduce the disciplines of reflection, contemplation, and meditation. With guidance and modeling, like the knight or the samurai warrior, young men will develop the self-discipline to undergo their own vigil. Note the importance of closing the eyes. Closing the eyes is important for two reasons. These exercises involve using the right side of the brain; light stimulates the left side of the brain. Denying light stimulus allows the right side of the brain to get into action. Also, as light stimulates the brain, denying that stimulus lets the brain "slow down."

Use these simple instructions for centering:

Sit comfortably in the chair letting it support you. Place your feet flat on the floor. Don't cross your legs or ankles as this interferes with your blood circulation. Let your hands rest on your lap. Keep your back straight. Close your eyes. Be still and concentrate on your breathing as you breathe in and out. Let your mind relax. Don't pay attention to any distracting noises or thoughts. Focus on your breathing and allow your body to relax. Breathe gently and deeply, in and out.

### Activity: Reflection Practice

Use the Centering Exercise to quiet the group and get them ready for the reflection practice. Then, use the following script:

- Think back over the day until you come to one positive experience. What made it positive? See the person, persons, places, or other things involved or present during this experience. Acknowledge them as blessing in your life. Be aware of the gratitude you feel.
- Now think back to another experience, an unpleasant or negative experience. What made this experience unpleasant or negative? Sit with this experience; don't be tempted to push it away. If this scene were to replay again what would you change or do differently? Maybe you could have avoided the unpleasantness; maybe you could not avoid the unpleasantness. Can you do something now or later to make this better? If you can, resolve to do it.
- Now think back to your moment of blessing. Bring this moment of blessing to the moment of unpleasantness. Let the feelings of blessing neutralize any negative feelings that remain. For these experiences and all the experiences of our day, let us say thank you. Amen.

## Activity: Contemplation Practice

Use the Centering Exercise to settle the group. Continue with the following instructions:

- Concentrate on your breathing. Gently follow your breath as you breathe in and out. Be aware of your body. If there are any parts of you that feel tight or discomfort, direct your attention there and breathe gently in and out.
- Be aware of your thoughts. Are they fast or slow? Don't try to think of anything; just be aware. Be aware of sounds around you—a fan, outside noises, noises from inside—but do not focus on any of them. Just be aware of them. Be aware of the chair or floor on which you are sitting, and breathe. With increased awareness of this moment, repeat the phrase silently and inwardly, allowing about three to five minutes to complete the activity. (Leader, choose one of the following phrases to give to the group.)
  - Blessed be God.
  - Jesus.
  - Jesus is Lord.
  - You have called me by my name, I am yours.
  - I am loved by God who is with me.
  - You have made me for yourself, my God.
  - Great is the Lord.
  - By the word of the Lord, all is made.
  - You are my hiding place O God.
  - The Lord is Faithful forever.
- Be aware of your breath as you gently breathe in and out.
- Be aware of your thoughts as you breathe in and out.
- Be aware of the sounds inside and outside as you breathe in and out.
- Gently open your eyes and be aware of all around you.

## Activity: Meditation Practice

Begin with the Centering Exercise. Continue with the following instructions as an introduction to the practice of meditation:

- Gently become aware of your breathing and notice its rhythm. Breathe slowly and deliberately without forcing your breath. Be aware of your thoughts. Do not concentrate on them. Gently let them go. As distracting thoughts come into your mind, do not focus on them but instead focus on your breathing. Specifically shift your focus to your breath just above your top lip. Keep your focus there as you gently breathe in and out. If your concentration shifts, gently bring it back, and focus on the breath just above your top lip and continue to breathe in and out. (Begin this exercise gently over no more than one minute and build its duration gradually to five or seven minutes.)
- Gently return your focus to the room. Gently stretch. Open your eyes.

## Alternative and Additional Activities

### Activity: Tonglen Contemplation

It is said that when Pope John XXIII opened the Second Vatican Council and welcomed the non-Christian delegates, he observed that the non-Christian religions had for a long time been a source of holiness for their peoples and that we had much to learn from them. Tibetan Buddhism practices a form of contemplation called Tonglen. This word means "loving-kindness" or "giving and receiving." In the Hebrew tradition, the word for loving-kindness is "hesed." As diverse as these religious traditions may be, they resonate with the Christian imperative to love one another (Matthew 22:39). This practice of love for one another obviously calls for actually doing acts of kindness for others. Contemplation can be employed as a spiritual act of kindness.

Tonglen is practiced for the benefit of others as an aid to spiritual growth. There are different ways to perform Tonglen. Often Tonglen requires visualization of another. Some ways to practice this as an exercise in contemplation might be to:

• Get the daily newspaper. Pick at random the name of someone who has died and pray for them.
• Pick someone with a large family, or a larger-than-average funeral notice, and give thanks for their life, even though we do not know them.
• Locate the funeral notice of someone with no or little family and pray for them.
• Pray for someone who has died, unknown, unmourned, and unloved.
• Locate a story in the paper of someone's misfortune and pray for them.
• Locate a story of someone's good fortune and pray with gratitude for their blessings.

# Rituals

## Overview

Rituals are ways to tell our sacred stories. In rituals we acknowledge the sanctity of our story by performing an action, saying something or by remaining quiet and still. Consider ritualizing something as simple as the beginning or ending to a gathering to mark out this time as special. What is significant about rituals is that, as they become established, they provide connection within individuals, between individuals, and with the world.

## Designing a Ritual

Use the following basic steps to custom design a ritual for any occasion or theme:

**1.** Prepare ahead by selecting Biblical readings, and opening and closing prayers that are appropriate. A good resource here is *150 Opening and Closing Prayers* by Carl Koch (Winona, MN: St. Mary's Press, 1990). Choose the music and prepare the space with candle(s), a Bible, a pot of sand and charcoal briquettes, and incense. Allow time before the ritual to light the charcoal so that it glows by the time the ritual begins.

**2.** Gather and quiet the group in preparation for prayer around the pot with the lighted charcoal heat beads.

**3.** Light the candle and recognize that it is the symbol for Jesus, who is always the light in our darkness.

**4.** Recite the chosen opening prayer.

**5.** Read the selected Scripture.

**6.** Call to mind our prayers in the silence of our minds and hearts.

**7.** One at a time, each participant comes to the pot with the charcoal. He takes one grain of incense and drops it onto the lighted coals in silent prayer, then returns to his place in silence.

**8.** Join together in "The Lord's Prayer."

**9.** Offer one another a sign of peace.

**10.** Close with a prayer of blessing. You may want to use one of the following:

**The Irish Blessing**
"May our neighbors respect us,
may trouble neglect us,
may the angels protect us,
and may heaven accept us"

or as St. Paul blessed the Ephesians

"Peace be to the whole community, and love with faith, from God the Father and the Lord Jesus Christ. Grace be with all who have undying love for our Lord Jesus Christ." (6:23–24)

## Tips for Good Rituals

The secret of creating good rituals is to get the boys involved or engaged. Although taking care not to turn the ritual into a performance by doing too many things, or having too much activity, involvement is crucial for participation. Some guidelines that are helpful in creating meaningful and prayerful experiences include:

- Keep a sense of balance. Punctuate activity with silence. Both are of value.
- Seek involvement of everyone. Don't automatically let the most extroverted members of the group "take center stage." Approach group members individually and let them know you would appreciate their help in making the rituals work. Thank them at the conclusion of the ritual.
- Find the time to plan your rituals. Give them thought. Don't stick to the one formula. What are the needs of the group at this time? What is going on in the world at the moment?
- Keep it simple. Quietness, stillness, and individually lighting candles between a couple of heartfelt prayers can have profound effects and provide the environment or building group trust.
- Lead by example. Bring your "self" not your role to prayer openly and honestly. Focus on your prayer life and trust God to use you as God wants.

### Activity: A Ritual for Contemplation

Rituals help us enter into mystery. In the following ritual boys learn this with a minimum of explanation. Emphasize the need for silence. This will focus the boys. Give instructions as necessary, but do not tell the boys the meaning of the activity. It is through their construction of meaning that comes the power of this ritual. This ritual may require two sessions.

**Preparation**
Gather the following supplies:
- 100 matches
- 1 tube of superglue or wood glue (All-purpose glue may not set quickly enough)
- Notebook paper or scratch paper to protect working surfaces and as a base for the individual structures

1. Give the following instructions to the boys:

   Working alone, create a structure with the supplies available. It can be any shape or form. Do your work on a sheet of notebook paper to protect the work surface. You are to work in silence. You will have about thirty minutes to create your structure.

2. Allow time and a safe place for the structures to dry. During the next session, day, or meeting time, gather in a circle sitting on the floor with each boy placing his construction in front of himself. Invite one boy at a time to move about the circle, looking at each structure in the circle. He should then return to his place and say something about his structure while the rest of the group listens. Repeat the process, allowing each boy about thirty seconds to observe other structures and another thirty seconds to speak about his own.

3. Move the group outdoors, with their structures, and again gather in a circle in silence. Tell the boys to light a match, set fire to their structure, and watch it burn. When all structures have burned, ask the boys to remain in total silence, turn away from each other, and record in their journals what they did, what they saw and what they learned. Allow twenty to thirty minutes for journaling.

4. Gather again in the circle. Take turns and go counterclockwise around the circle, giving each boy about one minute to describe his experience.

5. Sum up the activity along the following lines:

   This simple activity deals with profound mysteries. We see something arise in the imagination, take form, and remain only as ash or dust. We see an indication of the ephemeral or transient nature of things, including us. We watch matter turn into energy. We see something turn into nothing. The use of silence and the handling of something taboo like fire, gives an insight into the nature of ritual. This activity encourages us to wonder.

Adapted from *Uh-Oh* by Robert Fulghum (1991).
London: HarperCollins, pp. 77–78.

## Resource Materials

There are almost as many different types of prayer books as there are types of personalities. Different personality types have different preferences for styles of prayer. When working with adolescent boys, a range of resources will help meet a range of individual needs and preferences. Variety of style and format is good because it allows individual preferences to be met and also opens us to the richness of diversity. As Edward Hays has pointed out throughout *Prayer Notes to a Friend* (2002), "Jesus' instruction to 'pray always' (Luke 18:1) might just as well mean 'pray all ways' as 'pray constantly'" (p. 1).

Here are some suggestions for exploration of possibilities that can be used individually or collectively.

Hays, Edward. *Prayers for a Planetary Pilgrim: A Personal Manual for Prayer and Ritual.* Easton, KS: Forest of Peace Books, 1989. In my experience adolescent males enjoy exploring this prayer book. It has a wonderfully eclectic, forever-fresh collection of prayers for all occasions.

———. *Prayers for the Domestic Church: A Handbook for Worship in the Home.* Easton, KS: Forest of Peace Books, 1979. This is a wonderfully thematically organized collection of prayers for all occasions, many of which include useful suggestions for such things as pausing for silence, the lighting of candles, and addressing individuals. These invaluable suggestions prevent prayer from become lifeless.

———. *Prayer Notes to a Friend.* Easton, KS: Forest of Peace Publishing, 2002. This helpful little book is useful for anyone because it overflows with daily bite-sized tips and encouragements that affirm and remind the reader that prayer is our effort to raise our hearts and minds to God.

Mundy, Linus. *A Man's Guide to Prayer.* New York: Crossroad, 1998. With prayers gathered from many traditions, the author has assembled a collection of prayers that speak specifically to the needs of men.

O'Malley, William J. *Daily Prayers for Busy People.* Winona, MN: St. Mary's Press, 1990. This collection of prayers includes Scripture, traditional and modern prayers as well as inspirational thoughts. When working with a group, or working alone, pick up this book, open it at random and find inspiration for prayer.

Ramson, Ronald. *Praying with Frédéric Ozanam.* Winona, MN: St. Mary's Press, 1998. A different approach to prayer is to draw on one of the greats of our long, rich tradition, Frédéric Ozanam, founder of the Society of St. Vincent de Paul. This book is a way to journey with him, or invite him to journey with us. It encourages prayer in a process of growth that can be engaged individually or together as a group. There is something about the practice of Christianity, in working with the poor, that still stirs the idealism of young men.

Schreck, Nancy, & Leach, Maureen. *Psalms Anew: In Inclusive Language.* Winona, MN: St. Mary's Press, 1986. Praying the psalms in modern language and thought keeps our prayer life real. This volume provides ways to engage individuals and groups in further reflection and prayer on the Psalms.

Skehan, James W. *Praying with Teilhard de Chardin*. Winona, MN: St. Mary's Press, 2001. Similar to *Praying with Frédéric Ozanam,* this is a prayer pilgrimage, or journey, with one of the treasures of our rich tradition, as well as one of greatest mystics of the modern church. Whether marveling at the wonders of the cosmos or the wonder of something simple right before one's eyes, Teilhard de Chardin gently and constantly reminds us that the world is charged with the grandeur of God.

## Notes

Use this space to jot ideas, reminders, and additional resources.

# Coming to God in Prayer

## The Serenity Prayer

God, grant me the serenity to accept the things I
    cannot change,
Courage to change the things I can,
And the wisdom to know the difference.
Living one day at a time, Enjoying one moment at a
    time,
Accepting hardship as the pathway to peace.
Taking as He did this sinful world as it is, not as I
    would have it.
Trusting that He will make all things right if I
    surrender to His will;
That I may be reasonably happy in this life
 and supremely happy with him in the next. Amen.

## Love Is Born

Love is born
With a dark and troubled face
When hope is dead
And in the most unlikely place
Love is born:
Love is always born

Reprinted from *The Prayer Tree,*
by Michael Leunig
(North Blackburn, Australia:
HarperCollins Dove, 1991).
Copyright 1991 by Michael Leunig.
Used with permission.

## Prayer of St. Francis

Lord, make me an instrument of your peace.
Where there is hatred, let me sow love;
Where there is injury, pardon;
Where there is doubt, faith;
Where there is despair, hope;
Where there is darkness, light;
Where there is sadness, joy;
O divine Master, Grant that I may not so much seek
To be consoled, as to console,
To be understood, as to understand,
To be loved, as to love;
For it is in giving that we receive;
It is in pardoning that we are pardoned;
It is in dying to self that we are born to eternal life.

## Prayer of St. Augustine

"[B]ecause you have made us for yourself,
and our hearts will not be at peace
until they rest in you."

Reprinted from *Praying with Saint Augustine,*
compiled by Valeria Boldoni,
translated by Paula Clifford
(London: Triangle, 1987), page 40.
Translation and Introduction copyright © 1987
by The Society for Promoting Christian Knowledge.
Permission applied for.

**Part Two**

# Directions for Digging

Now that we have examined the tools for digging, we need to decide on the directions in search of what we seek. Socrates, the saints, heroes and villains, and most of the men we see every day have wrestled with the question, "Who am I?" Jesus has the answer to this question. He understood his identity, his true self, as the Son of God; and he saw us as his brothers and sisters. He invites us into a lifestyle that would encourage us to see like him. To understand what that means for us is to dig deep, exploring who we are by his light.

The light of Jesus also helps us wrestle with the big issues of masculinity, sex, and power. Both sex and power have the potential to make or break us as men. If they are not integrated into the wholeness of who we are, they will inevitably seduce and destroy the potential we seek.

Lastly, the relationship between a father and a son is most significant to who we are as men, and who we are as men of God. Whether our fathers are absent or present, known or unknown, it is a singularly significant relationship and it needs to be addressed if we are to learn to live authentically as men.

The exercises and activities in the following pages are a good way to make a start.

# Who Am I (Becoming)?

## Overview

"Who am I?", one of the oldest of all philosophical questions, is at the heart of male spirituality. Wrestling with the question leads to the discovery that the answer is bound up in a relationship with God and revealed in my daily experiences and encounters. The Trappist monk, Thomas Merton, recognized that spirituality was about discovering the "true self" (*Seeds of Contemplation,* p. 10). Our "true self" is obviously the truest reflection of the image and likeness in which we are made. But knowing for sure who our "true self" really is can be one of our greatest challenges.

Today we sometimes hear of people suffering "an identity crisis." This is not a modern phenomenon. The stories of Abraham, Jacob, Moses, and Jesus depict just a few of the many journeys of spiritual growth and maturing of boys into men. Each of these men had to wrestle with the question of their authentic identity in different ways. In each case, they come to realize who they are called to be. Their vocation, their calling to be their "true selves," was revealed in their daily struggles, joys, and disappointments. Their stories teach us that their identity was not in their jobs, social position or wealth. They each came to know their identity in relationship with God in the events that unfolded in their lives.

This chapter will first explore the question, "Who am I?" (and "Who am I not?") and then look ahead to the kind of men adolescent boys want to become.

## Pretense Versus Authenticity

"Getting your act to together" is a common phrase worth pondering. People say things like, "He has got his act together," or "He needs to get his act together." Consider the hidden meaning in the language that we use. If we are conditioned or encouraged to "get our act together" it might mean that we are encouraged to act with mindfulness, rather than thoughtlessness. However, this subtle message can also be misinterpreted, and as a result, we "act out" a role that is not authentically our "true selves."

Parker J. Palmer, in his volume *Let Your Life Speak: Listening for the Voice of Vocation* (San Francisco: Jossey-Bass, 2000), contends that most people spend the first half of their life being discouraged from acting out who they were born to be (p. 12). The problem starts before boys begin kindergarten. It seems there are innumerable subtle social pressures that get us to become everything but our true selves. As men, we have had a lifetime of training and conditioning so that we would not get too egotistical, too big for our boots. But a person's identity is a gift. It is what God has gifted a person, and creation, with. No wonder wrestling with the question "Who am I?" has always been central to the search for meaning in life.

## Activity: Pretending

### Preparation

○ Obtain the video *Grease* (Paramount Pictures, 1977, 1998) Beforehand cue video to 17 minutes after the opening credits. Write the questions to Step #3 on newsprint, the board, or photocopy on half-sheets of paper. Follow these steps:

**1.** Gather the group asking them to bring their journals. Give the following introduction to the movie clip:

    ♭ Danny and Sandy have started the senior year of schooling each unaware the other is attending the same high school. They meet and become friendly at the beach over the summer holidays. They both think that Sandy would be returning home to Australia, but at the last minute Sandy's plans change.

**2.** Play the video for several minutes and observe what happens when Danny and Sandy unexpectedly meet each other. Stop the clip, just after Sandy calls Danny "a phony" and walks off. Note the look on Danny's face.

**3.** Immediately following the clip, ask the group to respond in their journals to the video clip, using these questions:
- How does Danny feel when he first sees Sandy?
- How does he act when he first sees Sandy?
- How do his actions change?
- Why do his actions change?
- Do his feelings for Sandy change?
- How does Danny feel at the end of the scene?
- When was Danny his "true self"?

**4.** Bring the group together and discuss Danny's actions, using the following questions:
- When are Danny's actions a pretense? When is he "pretending"?
- Why does he react to his friend and then act differently towards Sandy? (Notice the word react literally means "to act again.")
- Identify the key relationships Danny negotiates. Explain the dynamics at work here.
- Why is it that some relationships influence and even override our own best interests at times?

**5.** Consider the view of the Canadian theologian Bernard Lonergan, that spirituality is about becoming more "authentic." (**Note:** The word "authentic" is similar in its origin to the word "author." In this sense, authors originate words for themselves and do not rely on others to "put words into their mouths."). Generate discussion with the group with the following questions:

- Do you think it is common for boys to act as "unauthentically" as Danny? Discuss the ways boys are encouraged to act in ways that are not their "true selves." What are the forces that conspire to encourage this status quo?
- How can Danny become more authentic?

**6.** Rewind the video (19 minutes) to the beginning of the first day at school and replay to the point where Sandy walks away from Danny. This time pay particular attention to the behavior of the boys. As a group, discuss the following:

- What do you notice about "boy behavior" in the movie?
- Is this typical of "boy behavior" in general?

**7.** Conclude this activity by having the group name at least ten recent movies with leading male characters struggling with the question, "Who am I?" How do they resolve this question in the movie?

## Activity: Authenticity

This activity is intended as a follow-up or second half to the previous activity, "Pretending."

**1.** Gather the group with their journals. Read out loud or write on newsprint or the board the Steve Biddulph quote that follows:

- ⚡ Steve Biddulph, author of *Manhood: A Book About Setting Men Free* (Sydney: Finch Publishing, 1994), begins his bestselling book with the following lines: "MOST MEN DON'T HAVE A LIFE. Instead, we have just learned to pretend. Much of what men do is an outer show, kept up for protection" (p. 1).

**2.** Have them respond to the following questions in their journals:

- What is Biddulph saying?
- Do you agree or disagree?
- Where are you not authentic? What works against authenticity for you?
- Where in your life are you authentic? Where in your life would you like to be more authentic? How do you become more authentic?

**3.** Come together into the circle and discuss this statement and follow-up questions among the group:

- ⚡ The theologian Bernard Lonergan suggests that spirituality is about becoming more "authentic."
  - ○ How does my spirituality impact my life and how does my life impact my spirituality?
  - ○ How can we support/encourage each other to be more authentic?

**4.** Conclude this activity by distributing copies of Handout 2-A, "A Prayer for Contemplation—Who Am I?" Before reading the prayer out loud or asking volunteers to read it, give the following information about the author of the prayer, Dietrich Bonhoeffer:

- Dietrich Bonhoeffer was born in Germany in 1906. He studied theology and spent time working at the University of Berlin before working in New York and London. Because of his views, Bonhoeffer came to the attention of the Gestapo in Germany in 1940. He was a pacifist but he worked with the resistance movement. He was implicated in a plot to murder Hitler and he was arrested in April 1943. While in jail he wrote what was later published as *Letters and Papers from Prison*.
- He was executed in early April 1945 shortly before the Allies liberated the prison camp where he was held.
- His well known prayerful reflection "Who Am I?" indicates his struggle with being his "true self." Bonhoeffer's words indicate authenticity; they indicate that the significance of his life and actions were likely to be as much a surprise to him as they have been inspirational to others.

## Who Am I Becoming?

The question, "Who am I?" leads to its corollary: "What kind of man am I becoming?" The activities in this section focus adolescent males on authentic role models who are worth emulating.

### Activity: Men We Admire

**1.** Gather the group in the sacred circle with their journals. Light a candle and settle the group to be attentive to a reading from Scripture. Ask a volunteer to read Genesis 18:16–33 aloud. After the reading, ask the boys to tell what they heard.

**2.** Introduce the concept of "a few good men" by paraphrasing the following:

We find the story of Abraham and God discussing the state of things in Sodom and what God is going to do about it. God has decided to destroy the city but Abraham pleads with God. Abraham asks if God will relent if Abraham can find fifty "good men" and God agrees. Abraham continues to bargain with God and eventually God agrees that if Abraham can find "ten good men," the destruction will not go ahead. Sadly Abraham cannot find ten good men and the destruction begins.

Sometimes in reading the newspapers, watching news reports, and just generally going through our day, we become aware that things in our world are not as they should be. Surely the violence, poverty, dispossession, and human misery evident on a world scale suggest that things are not as they are meant to be. Even in a relatively safe environment like ours, we see individuals burdened with loneliness, sadness, depression, family breakdown, and other misfortunes. Among all of this, can we come up with enough good men to make a difference?

Some writers and commentators would have us believe that men cause all the problems in the world. A look at our history reveals that it is men who wage war, the source of so much human misery and tragedy. The statistics that show that men are guilty of the majority of violent crimes, make up most of the inmates of prisons, and are responsible for the majority of family breakdowns. All this might lead us to believe that things are not all that different from the city of Sodom in the time of Abraham.

However, this type of thinking does not reveal the whole picture. It is misleading and unhelpful. Men are not the problem. Men who attend to their inner life, their spiritual life, hold the key to transforming the world.

If the scene from Genesis was played out here and now, and your task to avert destruction was to find ten good men, could you? How sure would you be? Where would you start?

**3.** Invite the group to journal on the following ideas and questions:

✍ Think of the men in your life. Like Abraham, you need to make a list of ten good men in your life or community. Write the names of these men in your journal. What are some of the qualities you admire in these men? Write the qualities alongside the men's names.

**4.** Gather the group into a circle and invite each boy to tell about one of the men on his list. Who are these men as individuals and what makes them notable?

**5.** After the boys have told about the men they listed, point out the variety of qualities that the men possess. This indicates that there is no "one way" to be a good man. The men identified may have characteristics in common but each one is unique. Likewise there is something about each of the young men present that makes them remarkable. They are growing into good men.

Before moving on to the next session, ask the boys, "Have you ever thought of telling one of the men you listed that you think that he is a good man?" If they haven't, follow up with "What's stopping you?"

## Activity: Qualities We Admire

### Preparation

Gather the following supplies:
- Make enough copies of Resource 2-A, "Qualities to Consider," so that each group of three to five boys receives one. Or, if you are working with a small group of less than ten, make a copy for each participant. You should also provide the following:
  - one scissors for each group
  - ten sheets of large newsprint, marking pens, and tape
  - sticky notes, enough for each participant to have five to ten notes

**1.** If you are working with a large group, use one of the techniques in chapter 1 to divide the boys into groups of four to six. Give each group or individual a copy of

Resource 2-A ("Qualities to Consider") and scissors. Give the participants these instructions:

- ℥ Cut out the individual characteristics along the scored lines, making a random pile. Starting with the boy in each group who has the birthday closest to Christmas, go around the circle clockwise with each boy selecting a characteristic from the pile. The group will discuss whether that quality is one that the group admires in a man. (**Note:** In smaller groups where each boy has his own copy, he can do this step alone.) Place the characteristic into one of four stacks:
  - ○ qualities we all admire
  - ○ qualities most of us admire
  - ○ qualities some of us admire
  - ○ qualities we don't admire

**2.** After all the characteristics are separated, the group should decide on any qualities that didn't appear on the list. Tell them to categorize these according to the four stacks. Starting with the qualities the whole group admires, they are to make a "top ten" list. Set this group of qualities apart from the others.

**3.** Gather again as a large group to develop the large group's "Top Ten Most Admired Qualities." Ask a volunteer to keep a tally on newsprint or the board as one group or boy leads off by giving their top ten characteristics. Using the results of all the groups, make a mark for the number of times that the quality appears. Count the marks to arrive at the overall top ten. They do not have to be prioritized.

**4.** Write the name of each of the top ten qualities in large letters across the top of a sheet of newsprint posted on the walls around the room.

**5.** In the large group, or back in the original small groups, tell the boys to come up with examples of men that they know personally or that they know about who display each of the characteristics. Encourage them to use specific examples, like "I really admire John at work. He is a good listener. If I go into his office, he always puts down his pen, stops what he is doing and he really listens to what I have to say. I admire this quality in him because it makes others feel valued."

**6.** Tell the group that this next step is to be done in silence. Give each group member five sticky notes and place the remainder in a pile in the center of the room. Ask the boys to think of the other young men in the room. Ask them:

- ℥ Who among us possesses the qualities we find so admirable? When you focus on one quality, whose face in the group comes to mind? Write his name on a small piece of paper and place that sticky note on the larger sheet naming the quality. Repeat until all small pieces of paper are used up.

**Note:** The facilitator should also participate in this activity, making sure that every boy's name is posted at one of the qualities.

**7.** Tell the boys to maintain their silence as they spend a moment or two silently focusing on what has become of the wall. What is it saying to this group?

**8.** Summarize by telling the group in your own words:

Quite often we are unaware of our own good points. Because they are "natural" we fail to notice them. Sometimes it is the qualities we have but are unconscious of, that we admire in others. We can spend our lives wishing we were someone else, when who we are really is good enough all along.

**9.** Distribute copies of Handout 2-B, "Created for Service," a prayer by Cardinal Newman. Tell the boys to reflect on what this prayer means to them, writing their response in their journals.

# Unseen Qualities

As we have grown in ecological awareness, we have recently come to appreciate what traditional cultures have always known. We do not just live in the world. We are part of the world. We interact with it in ways that are both conscious and unconscious to us. We affect our world, and our world affects us, whether or not we are aware of the interactions. Some of the things in our interactive environments are tangible, things like houses, trees, cars, and rivers. Other things in our environment are intangible, like the temperature, gravity, friction, music, and emotions.

One of the signs of our times is that we often forget that the nontangible things in our world are as real as tangible things. Traditional cultures were always conscious that the unseen things in life were just as real as the seen things. Even the ancient Greek philosophers, like Socrates, were consciously wrestling with the question, "How do I live a good life?"

Media images of men convey many messages about what it means to be a man today. As young men reflect on qualities they want to emulate, there are some characteristics that may remain "unseen." This section will dig deep to explore some of the less obvious treasures that reside within the hearts of men.

## Restlessness

"[Y]ou have made us for yourself, and our hearts will not be at peace until they rest in you" (Saint Augustine). Augustine calls it "restlessness," Ron Rolheiser names it "longing," Tom Zanzig uses the term "yearning," and the philosopher John Paul Sartre refers to it as the "hole in the soul." No matter what *it* is called, we often feel incomplete or a hunger for something more. Deep down, we know we are not there yet. The monk Thomas Merton said that what we long for is our "hidden wholeness." Often people are not conscious of what it is they yearn for; as a result, they spend their time and energy in getting things that won't satisfy themselves. When this happens, they search to satisfy the yearning, which goes on and on endlessly.

## Activity: The Young and the Restless

**1.** Write these two questions and points on a piece of newsprint posted on the wall or on the board:
- What is it that makes you restless?
- What do you long for?

**2.** Use some of the following examples to brainstorm with the group, posting everyone's answers:
- Better grades
- Acceptance by others
- A better body
- To be left in peace
- To have good friends
- To live in a nice house
- To have a car
- To have a better car
- To make the team
- To be acknowledged
- To feel at home

**3.** Tell the group to add to the group list in their journals. Allow about five minutes for writing, then ask them:
- What is it that males your age long for? Imagine you could grasp one of these things with each hand. Which two would you grasp if you could? Why these two?

**4.** As a group, decide which additions to include on the list and discuss why. After the group discussion, ask if anyone might change what they originally wrote in his journal.

**5.** Look again at the qualities listed by the group. On a separate piece of newsprint or the board, make two columns. Label them "Personal" and "Communal." Transfer what is recorded from the first piece of butcher's paper to the appropriate columns.

| Personal | Communal |
|---|---|
| Better grades | World peace |
| Acceptance by others | |
| To have friends | |
| To make the team | |

**6.** Gather the group into a circle and process the following with them: How do the two sides compare? Chances are that the "Personal" column will dominate. Explore this, asking why this is so and what does it mean?

**7.** Lead the group to make correlations between the columns. For example, the correlations may look like this chart:

| Personal | Communal |
| --- | --- |
| Acceptance by others | All people accept each other |
| To have friends | Everyone should have friends |
| To make the team | Everyone should feel included/ successful |
| To feel at home | All people should feel at home |
| To be acknowledged | Everyone is acknowledged |

**8.** Give the group the following information:

𝄢 Psychologists say that the state of the outer world is determined by the state of our inner world. They call this "projection"; we "project" onto the world what is going on inside us. The Buddha said something similar with his famous words, "With our thoughts we create the world." This is what Jesus meant when he said, "A good tree cannot bear bad fruit, nor can a bad tree bear good fruit" (Matt. 7:18). Likewise, he said, "what comes out of the mouth proceeds from the heart, and that is what defiles. For out of the heart come evil intentions . . ." (Matt. 15:18–19)

𝄢 The ancient Greek philosophers used the word "eudaimonia" to mean "happiness." This word also means, "human flourishing." Thomas Merton's "hidden wholeness," and the terms "flourishing" or "happiness" all refer to the same thing. Most spiritual writers and thinkers agree that the path to "happiness," "wholeness," or "flourishing" comes when transcending or overcoming selfishness and living for others.

One of the great mysteries of life is that the experiences of longing, yearning, and restlessness can have very different effects on people. Someone who knows loneliness can easily become insular, bitter, and selfish; or their loneliness can inspire them to look outside themselves and recognize and attend to the loneliness in others. Likewise, someone suffering injustice and inequality can become resentful, angry, aggressive, and intolerant of others; or they can strive for justice for all, not just themselves. This is one of the great secrets of life. We flourish and find happiness by devoting ourselves and our efforts for the happiness of others. Ultimately, we have a choice. We can choose to channel the energy from our experiences of longing creatively towards building up "the hidden wholeness" or we can let that energy continue its destructiveness on the outer world we live in.

**9.** Photocopy the following questions and ideas or post them on newsprint or the board. Invite the participants to reflect on these, writing their responses in their journals:

- Identify the parallels between the restlessness in your inner and outer worlds.
- What can you do with this restlessness? You may not be able to change the way others treat you, but you can resolve not to treat others similarly.
- Reflect on these passages from the Scriptures:
  - "God created humankind in his image, in the image of God he created them . . ." (Gen. 1:27)
  - "But I say to you that listen, Love your enemies, do good to those who hate you, bless those who curse you, and pray for those who abuse you." (Luke 6:27)

## Vulnerability

Is vulnerability an admirable quality for men? The word "vulnerable" comes from a Latin word that literally means "to enter into." One of the dangers of being a man is pretending that we are not vulnerable. To be human is to be vulnerable, both to relationships and the experience of love.

Vulnerability is not necessarily a weakness, but boys need to know otherwise. Young men need role models who are not afraid to admit their vulnerability. They also need safe places in which to be vulnerable. Without these, young men may not learn the valuable lessons of vulnerability and as a result have difficulty with intimacy in their most important relationships.

### Activity: Man Enough to Be Vulnerable

#### Preparation

- Obtain the video *Tuesdays with Morrie* (Harpo Films, 1999). Fast-forward the film to 64 minutes from the beginning. The scene begins with Mitch arriving at Morrie's house in the rain, and ends about eight minutes later with Morrie's words "we learn from what hurts us as much as from what loves us." Then follow these steps:

  **1.** Introduce the scene to the group:
  - The movie *Tuesdays with Morrie* is a true story about vulnerability and manhood. Morrie, a college professor, has become vulnerable to a disease that gradually makes him completely dependent on others. Morrie is dying, and over the last months of his life, he is visited by one of his former students, Mitch. Morrie has recognized that one day he will become completely dependent on others. When Mitch arrives for his visit, Morrie informs Mitch that this "landmark" day has now arrived.

  **2.** View the clip. Then ask the boys for their reaction, drawing attention to the following aspects of the scene:
  - Morrie says, "the culture teaches us that we should be ashamed" of dependency. He says that as an infant he was completely dependent on others; now that he is

dying, he is completely dependent on others. However, the secret is that in-between, we need each other even more.

- Morrie understands being spiritual as knowing that "we must love one another or die."
- Morrie believes that "we must learn from what hurts us as much as what loves us."

**3.** Rewind the video and play this scene again. Put the following questions on newsprint or the board, or photocopy the questions for members of the group, asking them to respond to one or more of the questions in their journals:

- In what ways does the "culture" teach us to be ashamed of our vulnerability?
- How do you react to Morrie's statement that between the helplessness of being an infant and of dying we are actually more dependent on each other?
- How does being dependent on one another make us vulnerable?
- In what ways do men pretend that they are not dependent and vulnerable?
- Morrie says that "we learn from what hurts us as much as what loves us." What are some things that hurt us and what do they have to teach us?
- Throughout the movie, Morrie quotes from a poem by W.H. Auden. In Auden's poem, "1 September, 1939," he writes "[W]e must love one another or die." What does this mean?
- Mitch refuses to admit his own vulnerability and as a result he does not allow himself the depth in relationships that he longs for. In his denial of his own vulnerability, he overcompensates by letting his life become over-busy. Para-doxically, Mitch's life is over full and empty at the same time. How do you relate to this kind of life?

## The Art of Husbandry

The skills of caring for, managing, and nurturing the flock are known as husbandry. Interestingly, the art of husbandry plays a significant role in the lives of men in the Scriptures. The skills of caring for flocks prepared men like Abraham, Jacob, Moses and David to lead God's people. Jacob and Moses were especially productive as managers of their flocks; their skills at husbandry must have been great because their flocks were fertile. Jacob's uncle Laban took it as a sign of God's favor with Jacob that he was able to nurture his flocks so productively.

However, not everyone thought of shepherds so highly. Their profession usually kept them outside or at the edge of town (Luke 2:8). Shepherds were definitely not in the "in crowd." In fact, they were disregarded by most. Yet, the first to be told of Jesus' birth were the shepherds (Luke 2:8–20).

There must be something about caring for sheep that makes shepherds men of God. In the Old Testament, there are several images of God as a shepherd (e.g., Psalm 23, Isa. 40:11, and Jer. 31:10), and Jesus refers to himself the "good shepherd" (John 10:11–16). After the Resurrection, Jesus asks Peter three times to take care of his sheep (John 21:15–17), reminding us that "the congregation of the Lord may not be like sheep without a shepherd" (Num. 27:17).

The activity below will explore the husbandry skills of nurturing and caring that Jesus modeled for his followers:

## Activity: The Elephant Man

### Preparation
○ Obtain and cue the movie video, *The Elephant Man* (EMI Films, 1980) to the scene beginning 100 minutes after the end of the opening credits.

**1.** Introduce the clip as follows:

♩ John Merrick, known as the Elephant Man because of his grotesque appearance, is victim of a disease we now know as "single gene disorder." Dr. Henry Treeves discovers John and writes about him in his journal. Dr. Treeves is initially interested in Merrick for purely scientific reasons, but the more he spends time with him, the more he begins to see John Merrick as a human being. Gradually the two men become friends. At the hospital where Merrick comes to live, a night porter physically abuses him. Merrick is abducted by a circus exhibitor, who considers him a freak because of his horrible deformity and he spends his time as an exhibit in a circus where he is again badly treated. Then one day, quite unexpectedly, the police find Merrick and bring him back to the hospital.

This scene from the movie is about three minutes long and it shows Merrick's return to the hospital followed by the conversation between Treeves and Merrick as they prepare for a visit to the opera.

**2.** Play the three-minute clip. Ask the group what they observed about Dr. Treeves.

**3.** Rewind and play the scene a second time, drawing the group's attention to Dr. Treeves' reactions to John Merrick.

**4.** Gather the group into the circle. Using the information just presented, explain to the group the concept of husbandry and its significance in the Scriptures along the following lines:

♩ Did you notice how Treeves showed his care for Merrick? There is something in our Scriptures about caring for the helpless and also about gathering lost lambs in our arms.

**5.** Follow this explanation with these questions:

♩ How is Dr. Treeves like a "good shepherd"? What are the skills of husbandry that he exhibits?

♩ How do men today (you and me) exercise these skills?

♩ In Jesus' time, he was being countercultural by telling his followers to develop the skills of nurturing, protecting, and caring. Is it still countercultural to expect men to develop these skills?

♩ The word "husbandry" is probably most associated with farming practices. However, the skills of husbandry seem applicable to the lives of men in general. Is there a particularly masculine way of nurturing that is different from feminine nurturing? What are the barriers that prevent men from developing the art of husbandry more fully?

**6.** Suggest the following as a topic for reflection in the boys' journals:
Reflect on the Scripture passage Isaiah 40:11 and how it relates to the scene from *The Elephant Man* when Dr. Treeves takes John Merrick in his arms.

## Life-affirming Images of Manhood

Where do we find good positive images of masculinity? Finding the theology in our stories will show us where to look. The more we are aware that we are never alone, that God is always close, the more we come to see what affirms life, and life to the full, all around us. Perhaps the image of the New York City fireman is one of the most respected images of masculinity in our present time. Although the average fireman is an ordinary man in so many ways, those with eyes to see can see much more. The next activity provides a good conclusion for this chapter. Consider incorporating it into a prayer service. Use the suggestions for designing a ritual in part 1 of this manual found on pages 37–38.

### Activity: Gentle Men Among Us

#### Preparation
Before this activity, do the following:
○ Locate one or more photos of New York City firemen at the scene of the tragedies of September 11, 2001. The image of the firemen carrying the body of Fr. Michal Judge is a particularly poignant one.
○ Photocopy the questions in step three.

**1.** Gather the group into a circle. Ask the group to describe what comes to mind when they picture a fireman.

**2.** Show the group one or more photos of the firemen in action on September 11.

**3.** Ask the group to respond in their journals to one or more of the following questions:
• In what ways does the image of the New York City fireman demonstrate the sacred art of husbandry?
• How does the image of the fireman help us understand a love story of a love so extravagant that it seems like foolishness to the worldly (1 Cor. 1:18)?
• How does the image of the fireman help us understand the vulnerability of manhood?
• Saint Paul says, "we are the aroma of Christ to God among those who are being saved and among those who are perishing" (2 Cor. 2:15). How does the image of the fireman help us understand what this Scripture means?
What do all these "signs of our times," events in our own time and place, have to say to us? We live in our own time and place where it is up to us to act for good. What sort of men are needed at this moment in the world's history?

**4.** Gather the group into a circle. Go around the circle and ask for each person's insights. What are some other positive life affirming images of manhood around us? What is God revealing to us through them?

# A Prayer for Contemplation: "Who Am I?"

**Who Am I?**
They often tell me I would step from my cell's confinement calmly, cheerfully, firmly,
   like a squire from his country house.
**Who am I?** They often tell me I would talk to my warders freely and friendly and
   clearly, as though it were mine to command.
**Who am I?** They also tell me I would bear the days of misfortune equably, smilingly,
   proudly, like one accustomed to win.
Am I then really all that which other men tell of?
Or am I only what I know of myself,
restless and longing and sick, like a bird in a cage,
struggling for breath, as though hands were compressing my throat,
yearning for colors, for flowers, for the voices of birds,
thirsting for words of kindness, for neighborliness,
trembling with anger at despotisms and petty humiliation,
tossing in expectation of great events,
powerlessly trembling for friends at an infinite distance,
weary and empty at praying, at thinking, at making,
faint and ready to say farewell to it all?
**Who am I?** This or the other?
Am I one person today, and tomorrow another?
Am I both at once? A hypocrite before others,
and before myself a contemptibly woebegone weakling?
Or is something within me still like a beaten army,
fleeing in disorder from victory already achieved?

**Who am I?**
They mock me, these lonely questions of mine.
Whoever I am, thou knowest, O God, I am thine.

Dietrich Bonhoeffer

Reprinted from *Letters and Papers from Prison,*
translated from the German by R.H. Fuller
(New York: Macmillan Publishing Company, 1963),
pages 18–20. Copyright © 1971 by SCM Press Ltd.
Reprinted with permission of Scribner,
an imprint of Simon & Schuster Adult Publishing Group and SCM Press Ltd.

# Created for Service

God has created me to do Him some definite service,
He has committed some work to me which He has not committed to another.
I have my mission—I may never know it in this life, but I shall be told it in the next.
I am a link in a chain, a bond of connection between persons.
He has not created me for nothing. I shall do good. I shall do His work.
I shall be an angel of peace, a preacher of truth in my own place,
if I do but keep his commandments.
Therefore, I will trust Him.
Whatever, wherever I am. I can never be thrown away.
If I am in sickness, my sickness may serve Him.
In perplexity, my perplexity may serve Him.
If I am in sorrow, my sorrow may serve Him.
He does nothing in vain. He knows what he is about.
He may take away my friends, throw me among strangers.
He may make me feel desolate, make my spirits sink, hide my future from me,
still He knows what He is about.

Cardinal John Henry Newman

Reprinted from *Treasury of the Catholic Church:*
*Two Thousand Years of Spiritual Writing,*
compiled by Teresa de Bertodano
(London: Darton, Longman and Todd, 1999), p. 190.
Copyright © 1999 by Teresa de Bertodano.

# Qualities to Consider

| | | |
|---|---|---|
| Accommodating | Competitive | Energetic |
| Active | Concerned | Faithful |
| Advantaged | Confident | Feeling |
| Aggressive | Contented | Forgiving |
| Agreeable | Controlling | Generous |
| Argumentative | Cooperative | Gentle |
| Assertive | Creative | Honest |
| Assured | Dependable | Honorable |
| Aware | Dependent | Hopeful |
| Balanced | Disagreeable | Humble |
| Careful | Dominant | Independent |
| Caring | Dutiful | Instinctive |
| Changeable | Emotional | Integrated |
| Communicative | Encouraging | Intimate |
| Compassionate | Excitable | Intuitive |

| | | |
|---|---|---|
| Judgmental | Possessive | Solid |
| Just | Powerful | Spiritual |
| Liberal | Practical | Spontaneous |
| Liberated | Proud | Strong |
| Logical | Rational | Submissive |
| Loving | Realistic | Talkative |
| Manipulative | Relational | Territorial |
| Masterful | Religious | Thoughtful |
| Merciful | Responsible | Tolerant |
| Mysterious | Restless | Tough |
| Nonviolent | Romantic | Trusting |
| Nurturing | Selfless | Unreliable |
| Objective | Sensitive | Violent |
| Open | Sensual | Visionary |
| Optimistic | Sentimental | Vulnerable |
| Pessimistic | Sexist | |
| Playful | Sexual | |

# Power in the Hearts of Men

## Overview

Power is invaluable when it truly serves a higher purpose. If power seduces, men wind up being enslaved to it. Power, anger, fear, anxiety, and rejection are all complex realities of life. Often young men do not deal with these issues well, and the consequences can be devastating.

Power in relationships is a bit like electricity. It can be of service for a better life or it can destroy. Just as it is essential to learn to use electricity wisely and to avoid the tragedy of its misuse, we must learn to use the power we experience in relationships for our own good as well as for others.

Likewise, when anger becomes channeled in healthy ways, it has the potential to improve relationships from family life to the global community. Much of the violence in the world is a projection of the unresolved anger inside many men. With wise guidance, boys can develop the necessary skills to constructively deal with anger and conflict.

### Power in Relationships

#### Activity: Relationships in Family

##### Preparation

○ Ahead of time the adult leader should draw a diagram of the dynamics of his own family of origin (see step 2). The diagram should be large enough for all participants to see.

**1.** Gather the group into the circle with their journals. Placing his prepared diagram in the center of the circle, the leader should explain his diagram, paying attention to the details as described in step 2.

**2.** In their journals, or on separate paper, ask the boys to draw diagrams of their own families, creatively illustrating the dynamics of power: conflict, closeness, alienation, and equality. They may want to use stick figures—with connecting lines that are dotted, solid, zigzag, wavy—or any other creative form of illustration.

**3.** Divide the group into smaller groups of three to five boys to discuss their diagrams. Post the following questions on newsprint or the board or photocopy them to guide the discussion (assure the group that they are not limited to these):

• Who holds power advantages over others in your family concerning areas such as: the remote control, the car, the food, the time, the bathroom, the kitchen, the yard, and the money?

• Who holds the power in relationships in areas like these: how the family spends free time, how the family gets along with each other, how the family prays or worships, decisions about education, and decisions about vacations?

• Who are the peacemakers or mediators? Are some people more into power games than others?

• Do males and females play power games differently? How? Why?

**4.** Give the group the following passage from Saint Paul's letter to the Ephesians: "I therefore, the prisoner in the Lord, beg you to lead a life worthy of the calling to which you have been called, with all humility and gentleness, with patience, bearing with one another in love . . ." (4:1–2) In their journals, they should respond to this question: What does this verse mean to you in terms of how we use power in relationships?

## Activity: Sibling Rivalry

Harold Kushner says that sibling rivalry goes all the way back to Cain and Abel (*How Good Do We Have to Be?*, pp. 120–121, 123). He points out that we all feel pain and anger whenever we suspect that someone else is loved more than we are. He says that even when parents don't actually play "favorites," we tend to think that the "other" is the favorite, not us, and this is what hurts. It is easy to think of our siblings as stealing love from us, when in fact, they probably feel as though *we* are the favorites, and not them. Kushner identifies this human condition as *original sin,* and says that coming to terms with these natural feelings of jealously are part of growing up.

This activity explores the age-old phenomenon of sibling rivalry among brothers. The activity will take about two hours to complete and easily adaptable to two sessions.

### Preparation

○ Put the names of these stories of sibling rivalry on index cards or slips of paper, along with their biblical references:

• Cain and Abel—Gen. 4:1–16
• Jacob and Esau—Gen. 25:21–34 and 27:1–45
• Joseph and his brothers—Gen. 37:1–36
• The prodigal son and his brother—Luke 15:11–32

**1.** Divide the participants into four groups, handing each group one of the slips or cards with the biblical story on them, a Bible, and a set of instructions found on Resource 3-A, "Sibling Rivalries: Tales as Old as Time"

There should be no more than about five participants in each group. Create more groups if necessary, duplicating one of the assigned stories. Give each group at least forty-five minutes to read their story and complete their tasks.

**2.** Return to the large group and draw straws to determine the order of the story-telling. Allow about ten minutes for each group's storytelling. Give kudos for each group effort.

**3.** After all of the presentations, discuss in the large group the role of competition in these stories and in the lives of men today. Discuss this statement and follow-up question:

Competition is often at the root of sibling rivalry and conflicts among men. When is competition healthy and when does it become destructive?

**4.** Conclude this activity by telling the group in your own words:

Because boys generally tend to compete more than girls, competition that escalates into conflict is more of a problem with boys. Therefore the growth of boys into fine men requires that they learn to connect rather than compete, so that they can delight in the good fortune of others. In doing this, they will get to experience delight. It will also help us in connecting, or relating with God, who is Love. This was Jesus' vision of the Reign or Kingdom of God: a place where all live as brothers and sisters in love-filled lives, knowing that God loves them endlessly. This would enable us to live lives of extravagant loving, never fearing that there would not be enough left over for us.

**5.** Invite the boys to respond in their journals to the following question: What sort of brothers are we called to be for the sake of the Kingdom? How does this brotherhood extend beyond our families to society?

## Power of Anger

Sigmund Freud drew upon the Greek myth presented by Sophocles about an angry young man called Oedipus to explain the journey from boyhood to manhood. Oedipus appears to be a victim of his circumstances born into a "no-win situation." At birth, a seer predicted that he would grow up and kill his father. Trying to escape his fate, Oedipus runs away from what he thinks is his home. Along the road, he comes to an impasse on a bridge with another man, a stranger whom he does not recognize as his real father. In this ancient incident of road rage, Oedipus winds up killing the man he does not realize is his real father, thereby sealing his fate as predicted.

To Freud and others who observed the world, this myth made sense of a world in which young lions grew up to kill their fathers and took over until the next generation of younger, stronger lions took over in their turn. Such is "the law of the jungle."

Anger is a natural human emotion. It is neither good nor bad. We cannot deny anger. It is part of our experience of life. Men need to know and understand anger, rather than repress it. Instead of Oedipus and his father, who could not control their rage, we have the model of Jesus, who took the lead from his Father, who is always "slow to anger." If the two men in Sophocles' tragedy had acted differently at their encounter, tragedy could have been averted by both of them. Jesus showed us that violence is never the answer. Although God's plan for us is for peace not disaster, we must choose "truth and action"(1 John 3:18) to play our part cooperatively. Whether leaders of nations, or two males coming face to face at an impasse, how we deal with our anger is a choice we need to make wisely.

## Activity: Myth of Redemptive Violence?

This activity will consider the myth of "redemptive violence . . . the story of the victory of order over chaos by means of violence" (Walter Wink, *The Powers That Be*, p. 48). From our most ancient myths to contemporary literature and film, there are myriad examples of evil and violence being vanquished by good. The myth of "redemptive violence" is played out in the structure of children's cartoon shows, comics, video and computer games, and movies. We also encounter it in the media, in sports, nationalism, militarism, and foreign policy. Violence's orientation toward evil is one into which virtually all modern children (boys especially) are socialized in the process of maturation (see also *www.webedelic.com/church/winkf.htm*).

The trouble with this thinking is that there is no such thing as redemptive violence or violence used for good. Violence and aggression is always wrong and it is always self-destructive. The Gospel command is that we do not repay violence with violence; instead, we should love our enemies and pray for those who persecute us (Matt. 5:44). Of course, this way of thinking is contrary to popular thinking. Violence is so seductive as a solution to the violence we encounter in the world that the people who advocate meeting violence with nonviolence are as likely as Jesus to wind up crucified. What does this say to us as men?

**1.** Gather the group and tell them that they need to literally "take a stand" on violence. Point to one corner of the room, and say:

> ⚡ In this corner, we have the opinion that violence is always justified and may be good. In the opposite corner we have the opinion that violence is never justified and always an evil. Between these two corners, we have a continuum or sliding scale. Everyone now needs to take a stand on how they view the use of violence to solve conflict.

Once group members are in position, ask them to sit with two other boys closest to them, staying close to the place where they stood. They are to discuss with each other why they have chosen their position on the continuum. Allow about five minutes for discussion.

**2.** Working from the extremes of continuum, alternating between the far ends, and working toward the center, give each group a chance to state their thoughts. Be careful to model tolerant listening. Ask clarifying questions, like:

> ⚡ How are our opinions on topics like this formed? What are the most significant factors that inform our thinking about ways to solve conflict? Why do you think we are like that?

**3.** In your own words, explain the "myth of redemptive violence" using information from the narrative just described.

**4.** On the board or large newsprint, brainstorm with the group, listing examples of movies, video or computer games, and comics that illustrate the concept of redemptive violence. Have volunteers explain how these examples perpetrate the myth that violence is a good way to resolve conflict.

**5.** Repeat the step above, listing examples that portray nonviolent ways of addressing the problems of injustice. The group may have a difficult time thinking of any. One example is *Ghandi* (Columbia/Tristar Studios, 1982). This is a long movie, but it does illustrate active nonviolence as an effective neutralizer of violence. Explore with the group the reasons why there are so few examples in history, literature, or popular entertainment that promote Gandhi's approach. Cite the examples of Martin Luther King, Oscar Romero, and Nelson Mandela.

**6.** As a journal exercise, give the group the following quote by Gandhi:
⅔ "An eye for an eye makes the whole world blind." What did he mean? Can you see examples of this in our world today? What is the alternative? Journal your responses to these questions.

## Activity: Responses to Anger

**1.** Gather the group, centering them to prayerfully listen to the Scriptures. Read aloud the story of Moses in the scene when he kills an Egyptian who was beating a Hebrew slave (Exod. 2:11–15). Remember that Moses, a Hebrew, had been raised in the court of Pharaoh.

**2.** After the reading, have the group journal a response for five minutes, recounting the facts of the story and what may have been going on inside Moses' head and heart as he killed a man. Respond to the questions: "Which parts of the story do I resonate with?" and "What does this story say to me today?"

**3.** Regather the group to discuss the story, using the responses in their journals as a catalyst. Explore the connection between Moses' outer world and his inner world. Draw two columns labelled "outer world" and "inner world." List the facts of what was going on in the story under the "outer world" heading and the thoughts and feelings of Moses under the "inner world" heading. Possible answers under the "outer world" heading might include the following:
• He saw something happening that wasn't fair.
• He got angry and he lashed out violently.
• He saw the Hebrew slave powerless.
• He saw the Egyptian abusing his power.
Under the "inner world" heading, use examples such as the following:
• He let his own power run out of control.
• He did not think first of the consequences of his actions.
• He was afraid of getting caught.

**4.** Continue the discussion, asking the group to respond to these questions:

§ Place yourself in Moses' position. Think of why he got so upset on seeing the abuse of the slave. He was raised as an Egyptian—why did he care?

§ As the "son" of Pharaoh's daughter, he would have had some influence. Why didn't he use the authority he had?

§ He must have seen a lot of things that were unfair. Why couldn't he deal with this one calmly?

§ Might he have been in the habit of hurting others when he got angry?

§ Living in the palace, is it possible that he might never have learned to take responsibility for his actions?

§ Did he confuse "acting tough" with being strong?

**5.** As a follow-up to the discussion, give the group the following information:

§ Later, as a man, Moses was wiser. He did not respond to the Pharaoh's unjust and unreasonable treatment of the Hebrews with violence and aggression (Exod. 5–12:29). Although he was constantly provoked, Moses did not respond in kind. He relied on God who he had learned to trust. Justice came to Pharaoh but not as vengeance from Moses and his people. Ultimately, Pharaoh suffered as a consequence of his own actions.

In the Eastern religions like Buddhism and Hinduism, we find the concept of "karma" (sometimes called "karna"). Karma is a spiritual energy that flows as a consequence of our actions. It can be either positive, negative, or neutral. Karma is like a boomerang in that it ultimately returns to the one from whom it came. Buddhists and Hindus believe that if you do good, good spiritual energy will come back to you. Likewise, if you do bad things, bad spiritual energy will ultimately flow back to you. It is a bit like the old sayings, "Sooner or later all your chickens come home to roost," and "What goes around comes around."

**7.** As a journal exercise, suggest that the boys reflect on the story of Moses in light of their own experience, using the following visualization and reflection:

• Go back over the scene that was played out with Moses. What do you think he should have done? How do you think you might have played out those same events?

• What makes you angry? What makes you so angry that you don't deal with it well?

• How do you experience injustice?

• Who do you hurt when you get really angry? In what ways do you hurt others when you're really angry?

• How do your actions escalate or deescalate angry situations?

• When you "control" your anger, do you feel better or worse?

### Alternate Activity

Have someone prepared beforehand and ready to talk personally about dealing with anger. This may be one of the group leaders or a visitor to the group. Invite a guest speaker. Some groups able to provide visiting speakers are listed in the resources at the end of this chapter. The talk needs to be honest. Anger or "rage" is a natural experience of growing up. Boys will only learn to deal with anger by talking honestly "man to man." Ask the speaker to focus the talk on the following ideas:

Sometimes we just have to accept that life is not fair and we have no choice but to live with it. We must learn to keep perspective. Sometimes we have to realize that what makes us angry really doesn't matter that much. Being strong and acting tough is not the same thing. Sometimes being strong enough to take it means that we stop the situation from escalating.

## Activity: Another Approach to Anger

**1.** Read and reflect on the story of Jesus and the woman caught in adultery (John 8:1–11).

**2.** Discuss the following points:
- How did Jesus defuse the anger of the angry mob?
- Why did he stay sitting on the ground during this ordeal?
- How might this situation have been different if Jesus responded to the angry mob in anger?
- What was Jesus doing by writing on the ground and avoiding eye contact with the members of the angry mob?
- What do you imagine the mob would have been muttering to Jesus as they walked away?
- How do you think Jesus was left feeling as the mob reluctantly walked away?
- Was Jesus focused on his own humiliation or the woman's?
- The crowd was no doubt full of "tough guys." What do you think they thought of Jesus?
- Is it possible that there were men in the angry mob who really didn't want to be there, but they weren't strong enough to stand apart?

**3.** Suggest the following question for a journal reflection:
- What does this story teach me about the way I deal with my anger?

## Alternate Activity: *October Sky*

**Preparation**
○ Obtain and preview the film *October Sky* (Universal Studios, 1999). Prepare a short summary of the plot. Cue the movie to the scene about forty-five minutes into the movie where Homer and his friends are arrested at their high school.

**1.** With a group of boys, play the scene to the point when Homer, his father, and his friend drive off in the car together.

**2.** Tell the boys to focus on the responses of Homer's father and his friend's stepfather to the boys' arrest. Then ask the following questions to highlight different approaches to anger:

- How angry was Homer's father with the stepfather?
- Why didn't Homer's father treat the stepfather the way the stepfather treated his stepson? Revisit the debunking of the redemptive violence myth in the "Redemptive Violence?" activity on page 65.

**3.** Replay the scene again. This time get the boys to focus on Homer's feelings. Homer had been unjustly accused and couldn't prove his innocence. He was subject to his father's disappointment in him. Focus on Homer's face as the three drive off in the car. He looks at his father differently.

**4.** Give the participants the following questions to respond to in their journals:
- What is Homer thinking about his father?
- What has his father taught him (without saying a word)?
- What do we learn from the two men about the difference between being strong and "acting" tough?
- Which of these men in this scene is the strongest?

## Ritual: Harden Not Your Hearts

Use these suggestions for creating a simple ritual. For more extended prayer service, check out ideas for ritual in part 1 of this manual, pages 37–42.

### Preparation

○ Write the following Scripture passages below along with their corresponding number on slips of paper. If the participants do not each have their own Bible, make sure one is available for the ritual.
- Isa. 6:8–10
- Psalm 95:8–9
- Matt. 13:10–15
- Heb. 3:7–8
- James 1:19–21

**1.** Gather the group in a circle around a lit candle. Hand out slips of paper to volunteer readers.

**2.** Beginning with the slip of paper marked number "one," ask the volunteers to prayerfully read their assigned passage. Pause a minute between readings.

**3.** Tell or read the following story:
♪ There is a story of a wise Native-American chieftain who said to his grandson, "I have two animals inside me. One wants to nurture and protect, the other wants to take revenge and destroy. They are constantly fighting each other."
"Which one will win, Grandfather?" asked the boy.
"The one that I feed, grandson."

"Two Wolves," author unknown

**4.** Sit with the story in silence for about a minute, then invite the group to offer comments or insights about the story. Use these ideas as points of discussion:

- What does it mean to be "hard hearted"? (*Answer:* Hard-hearted means that there are some things we become blind and deaf to.)
- How do we feed the two animals inside of each of us? How does this happen in our communities, our church, our nation, and the global community?
- Why is there a recurring call in these passages from Scripture to "harden not our hearts"?

**5.** Offer prayers of petition like the ones that follow, and encourage others in the circle to offer similar prayers:

- Lord, please give me your grace in my life so that I . . .
- Father in heaven, open my eyes where I am blind to . . . and help me to find the courage to . . .
- God, in my community, please help me overcome my deafness to the struggles of . . . and help me be a channel of your love by . . .

**6.** Say the Lord's Prayer together.

**7.** Offer each other a sign of peace.

## Resource Materials

### Print

Wink, Walter. *The Powers That Be.* New York: Galilee Doubleday, 1998. This book is very readable and addresses complex issues with clarity, throwing much light on how insidiously violence weaves its way into our everyday interactions. Our world would be a much less violent place if we encouraged men, young and old, to read and internalize the wisdom Wink has to offer in this text.

### Internet

The University of Lethbridge, Violence in Schools Web site (*www.edu.uleth.ca/ students/Ed4321Projects/studentpages/Violence/Case.html*) considers the causes of violence in schools and the impact of violence on television.

The Phoenixville Area Violence Prevention Network has a list of programs and useful links to other Web pages for numerous sites at: *www.pavpc.com/consumers. htm#Helpful.*

A Canadian project has some good advice for "Transition to Adolescence, Strong Social Skills" at: *www.growinghealthykids.com/english/transitions/adolescence/ social_skills_pgs/content.html.*

The classic Catholic document on peace in the world, *Pacem in Terris* by Pope John XXIII, is available at the social justice Web site: *www.osjspm.org/cst/pt.htm.*

Each paragraph would make a wonderful stimulus for discussion.

United States Conference of Catholic Bishops, *Renewing the Mind of the Media* (Statement on Overcoming the Exploitation of Sex and Violence in Communications from the U.S. Catholic Bishops). Washington, DC: 2002. This publication addresses the "gratuitous violence and misuse of sexuality" in the media.

## Other

Some suggestions for help in obtaining visiting speakers can be found by visiting the Alcoholics Anonymous Web site at: *www.alcoholics-anonymous.org/* and the Narcotics Anonymous World Service web site at: *www.na.org/*. These groups can also be contacted by phone. Their phone numbers are listed in the telephone directory.

*From Rage to Reason Board Game.* Players earn play money by giving "Randy" good advice on how to deal with frustrating and anger-provoking situations throughout the day, both on the job and in personal life. "Randy" is rejected by a friend, taken advantage of by a coworker, and suffers through other anger-provoking situations typical of older teenagers and young adults. Available from Jaguar Educational, *www.jaguared.com,* 877-524-4885.

## Notes

Use this space to jot notes, ideas, reminders and additional resources.

# Sibling Rivalries:
# Tales as Old as Time

You have 40 minutes to complete the following tasks:

**1.** Select one member of your group to read your assigned story out loud. Although the story may be familiar, listen for details that you may not have heard before.

**2.** After the reading, sit for three minutes in silence, letting the story sink in. Write in your journals any insights or questions that come to you in the silence.

**3.** As a group, discuss the following questions:
- Describe the personalities of the main characters in the story.
- How important is the role of the father in this story?
- Is the favoritism experienced by the sons real or imagined?
- What does this story say to us about relationships in families?

**4.** As a group, your mission is to tell this story to the large group in a creative way, using every member of the group in some capacity. You may not change the major details of the story, although you may choose to use a modern setting and contemporary language and references to bring the story alive. Use props, music, art, or any other creative elements to enhance the storytelling. Your retelling of the story should not exceed ten minutes.

# Sacred Sexuality

## Overview

This chapter will explore sexuality as a sacred aspect of masculinity. To be human is to be a sexual being, a significant dimension of the holy image and likeness of God. Because of its sacredness, energy, and power, there are many cultural taboos regarding sexuality. As a result, we live in a culture that either does not approach sexuality with ease, or else approaches it too easily, without due reverence. Neither of these approaches honors the grace of this God-given gift that is integral to who we are.

Remember that boys need men to initiate them into the sacred conversations of manhood and that many males have not had the opportunity to discuss sex in a way that is healthy and life-giving. Know that adolescent males hold a deep yearning to have this conversation. But be aware that when *talking* about sex in a serious venue, teenage boys will most likely be slow to respond. Honor this yearning with patience, even though the waiting time may seem to drag on forever. Don't force it. Once they begin, the conversations will flow. Listen carefully as participants open up.

This overview is good preparation for you and any other men (including fathers of participants) who will be involved in conversations about sacred sexuality. Consider inviting mature men from the parish or community to be a part of these conversations as role models or as experts in a particular aspect of sexuality, including biological, psychological, or theological issues into the discussion.

- Talk with the boys, not at them. Ask clarifying questions but avoid sounding moralistic.
- The aim is to be respectful; this conversation is about respect for self and the other. We must constantly model this for each other.
- All present must be clear as to what the boundaries are and draw the lines firmly so the conversations are appropriate.
- This is not a biology lesson. However, questions of body, mind, and spirit all contribute towards wholeness.
- There are some things so sacred they cannot be spoken. Acknowledge this. It not only models respect, it also models that a man does not have to pretend to have all the answers all the time.

## Dimensions of Sexuality

The activities in this section will introduce the topic of sex and sexuality as integral to who we are as persons made in the image and likeness of God. The activities focus on the distinction between sex as a genital activity and sexuality as the God-given energy by which we relate to others physically, emotionally, and spiritually.

### Activity: Defining Sex and Sexuality

The purpose of this exercise is to get comfortable talking freely and naturally about sexuality, and to distinguish genital sexuality from sexuality in general.

### Preparation
○ Obtain pieces of large newsprint, markers, and a set of index cards so that there is at least one for each person in the group. Write out the questions in Step #5 on a large piece of newsprint. Have available blank sheets of newsprint.

**1.** Gather the group into a circle. Ask each alternate boy to face outside the circle. Hand out the index cards so that each person present has one.

**2.** Ask each person to anonymously write down something they would like clarified or discussed about sexuality. Ask every person to write something, even if it is a few lines from a nursery rhyme. (This will guarantee anonymity of the individuals present.) Tell them that you will review their questions and will address them in future sessions. Encourage them to continue to submit questions either verbally or on the index cards. Designate a box or place for these to preserve confidentiality. Set aside time at the beginning or end of each session to pull a few cards and respond to the questions.

**3.** In the center of the group, place a large piece of blank newsprint and some markers. Ask for a volunteer scribe to write down the insights raised by the group. Have the scribe write the word "SEX" on the top of the paper. Give the following instructions to the group.

  ⸮ What are the different meanings of the word "sex"? When the word "sex" is mentioned, people often forget the complexity and variety of meanings carried by that one word. Most people often immediately think of sexual activity involving the genitals, which is only one small part of a person's sexuality. As a group, brainstorm the multiple meanings of the word as the scribe writes them down.

  **Note:** This list provides possible answers, without being prescriptive or exhaustive:
  - sexual intercourse
  - sexual arousal and stimulation
  - distinction between male and female
  - separating a group of organisms into males and females
  - sexual matters raised in conversation
  - ways specific to being male or female

**4.** Post the list in full view of the group.

**5.** Next to this list, post the prepared newsprint with the following questions. Consider playing some gentle instrumental background music. Ask group members to journal responses to the following questions for ten minutes:
- What does sexuality mean?
- In what ways is masculine sexuality more straightforward than feminine sexuality?
- What is it about masculine sexuality that is more complicated?
- Why is it awkward or difficult to talk comfortably about matters of sexuality?

**6.** Ask for volunteers to share their thoughts on the questions. Allow about ten to fifteen minutes for discussion. If no one speaks for the first few moments, don't panic. Just sit and wait patiently for a response. Casually look at each of the group members without pressuring anyone; be mindful with your body language or facial expressions. Don't feel obliged to fill the silent space with words, even though the waiting time will seem to drag on forever. Once they begin, the conversations will flow. As you listen to the responses of group members, ask clarifying questions. This is an opportunity to begin a conversation that too many males do not have, in a way that is healthy and life-giving. Note any items of concern, recurring issues, and levels of comfort and knowledge within the group. The questions on index cards and the conversations are part of intelligence gathering, to help inform you of the aspects of sexuality that are most in need of addressing.

**7.** To conclude this activity, say in your own words:

♫ Most aspects of sexuality are not about genital sexuality but about expressing a unique gift, the gift of our sexuality. As human beings, made in God's image, our bodies, minds, and spirits cannot be separated or compartmentalized. Since our sexuality is a part of being human, it has physical, psychological and spiritual dimensions as well. The wholeness—or the holiness—of sexuality balances and integrates all three of these dimensions. Sexuality cannot be separated from who we are. We express our sexuality in how we relate to others in our daily lives as we talk, walk, play, laugh, and cry. It is not something expressed only, or even primarily, in genital ways.

If sexuality is part of who we are, then its energy involves relationships of all kinds: physical, emotional and spiritual, including our relationship with God.

The term "sex" often implies genital activity. As a dimension of our sexuality, the purpose of genital activity is not just physical pleasure, but also the creation of life and the expression of committed love with another person.

## Male and Female, We Are Created in God's Image

Although the words "male" and "female" describe our physical gender, the terms "masculine" and "feminine" refer to characteristics that have typically been associated with men or women. Masculinity and femininity express differences that, together, reflect the wholeness of God. Coming to appreciate the masculine and feminine characteristics of God, ourselves and others leads us to the wholeness of sacred sexuality.

## Activity: Images of God

### Preparation
○ Have available several large sheets of newsprint, markers, and a Bible.

**1.** Divide the group into smaller groups of three or four. Give each group a large sheet of newsprint and a marker. Give the following instructions:

　 ♪ The first task of your group is to select a scribe who will take notes as the group brainstorms to create a list of images of God. Remember the prohibition of the second commandment about limiting God to an image, as if carved in stone. This means we are to free our mind to know God in the infinite ways God wishes to be revealed to us. You have ten minutes to create your list.

**2.** Give each group a clean sheet of newsprint and instruct the scribes to make three columns down the length of the sheet with these headings from left to right: masculine, masculine and feminine, and feminine. Instruct the groups to look at their original list, then transfer the images to the appropriate columns. As they finish, have them post their lists on the wall for the large group to view. Give them ten minutes to process this task.

**3.** Ask the boys to take five minutes of silence to observe the lists posted around the room. Then bring them back to the large group to discuss any insights they had from the process. Consider the following questions:
• Was it difficult to assign gender characteristics to an image of God?
• Are there any surprises in the posted lists?
• Do you agree with the placement of all the images. Would you move any?

**4.** Post a clean sheet of newsprint with the three headings at the top: masculine, masculine and feminine, and feminine. In the large group, make a general list of images of God based on the small group lists. Beginning with the images that were listed most frequently, transfer the images to the clean sheet under the appropriate headings. Indicate the number of times the image appeared among the groups. Make sure to include all images, even if they are used only once. If the images were listed under different headings in the small groups, come to a large group consensus about where they belong. If consensus is difficult, explore the question: "Why are gender labels difficult to assign when talking about God?"

**5.** Give volunteers individual slips of paper or index cards with the following Scripture passages:
• Deut. 32:11–12
• Psalm 131:1–2
• Isa. 49:15
• Isa. 66:13
• Matt. 13:33
• Luke 13:35
• Matt. 23:37

Ask individuals to look up the passage on their paper, reading it aloud to the group. After each passage is read, ask the group what image of God do they hear described. If the image is not already listed on one of the newsprints, add it under the appropriate heading.

**6.** Focus the attention of the group to the last two Scripture passages where Jesus refers himself to a mother hen. "Why does Jesus refers to himself like a mother hen?" Consider the responses, challenging the group to wrestle with such questions as, "Why did not Jesus say, 'as a rooster gathers his chicks'?" Ask them if they consider that Jesus was ambiguous or assured in his sexuality as a man. Obviously, if Jesus had such a constant and significant effect on those who come in contact with him, he must have been quite together, integrated, and balanced, especially about issues of identity.

**7.** Ask the group to spend ten minutes pondering this question and responding to it in their journals:

> If God did not want the Divine image to be limited by limited forms of expression, and we are made in God's image, then might it follow that expression of our own sacred selves cannot be limited to fixed forms?

## Activity: Gender Qualities

If both men and women are made in the image of God, and God cannot be held to gender stereotypes, what does this mean for us as men? This exercise builds on the previous exercise to recognize and unpack gender stereotypes. It also reinforces the concept that sexuality is much more than genital sexuality.

### Preparation
○ Make enough copies of Resource 2-A, "Qualities to Consider" on pages 60–61 of this resource manual for each group of three to five to have one copy. Each group will also need scissors, glue, and newsprint.

**1.** Form groups of three to five boys. Give each group a copy of Resource 2-A, "Qualities to Consider," scissors, glue and a large sheet of newsprint. Give them these instructions orally or in writing:

> In the previous activity, we tried to determine which images of God fit into "masculine," "feminine," and "masculine and feminine" categories. We will do the same with human qualities. Draw the three columns lengthwise on the newsprint, labeling them as "masculine," "masculine and feminine," and "feminine." Cut the characteristics into individual slips, then glue them in the appropriate space on the newsprint. If there are qualities that your group cannot agree upon, do not glue them to the newsprint, but set them aside. When your group is done, post the list on the wall.

**2.** Ask the boys to observe one another's lists, noting the differences. Return to the large group with any unassigned qualities. Starting with the leftover qualities (if there are any) discuss any controversy that came up in the groups about the placement of qualities. Which qualities were the most difficult to place?

**3.** Provide the following information:

𝄞 Some psychologists and mythologists identify **archetypes** as recurring patterns or expressions of the human psyche across cultures and time. In some cultures, the Sun represents male energy or masculinity, while the Moon represents female energy or femininity. In many Asian cultures, this duality of masculine and feminine principles is sometimes represented by two fish connected head to tail. In European culture the Maypole, a feminine ring surrounding a masculine pole, also expressed this archetype. Perhaps the most widely recognized expression of the masculine and feminine archetype is the *I-Ching* symbol known as Yin-Yang. So regardless of the culture or time of origin, it seems that in almost all cultures masculine and feminine energy is recognized as different but complementary. Each culture represents this with relevant symbols.

**4.** Lead the large group in a discussion about the benefits or risks of consciously or unconsciously labeling these qualities masculine or feminine. The following questions may be useful as a guide:

- What is the effect of gender stereotyping of qualities such as these?
- How valid is it to restrict these qualities, such as being rational, compassionate, or emotional, to being either masculine or feminine?
- How might conscious or unconscious stereotyping such as this might disadvantage females?
- Explain how males might also be disadvantaged by this type of gender stereotyping. Encourage group members to raise other insights and questions about the significance of gender stereotyping.

**5.** Provide the following perspective as a follow-up to this discussion:

𝄞 A healthy perspective reveals that within each female lies a masculine dimension and within each male lies a feminine dimension. A whole and healthy person is aware of each dimension within himself: "Jesus demonstrated in his humanity what it means to embrace both the masculine and feminine sides of our nature. He exhibited qualities typically and culturally attributed to both genders. He was nurturing, sensitive, compassionate, and intuitive. He wept at the death of his friend Lazarus (John 11:32–36) and expressed concern for the care of his mother (John 19:26–27). He was also forthright, logical, intellectual, and brave, often challenging authority. He confronted the gender issues of his day when he included women in his inner circle and conversed with them in public. In short, Jesus acted as the situation demanded, drawing from the full repertoire of his human sexuality." (Clare VanBrandwijk, chapter 9 of *Called to Covenant*, Winona, MN: Saint Mary's Press, 2004.)

**6.** Play some gentle background music and invite the group to journal their responses, questions and insights from this activity for ten minutes. Provide the following questions for reflection:

𝄞 Where do we make assumptions about what is masculine and what is feminine in our daily relationships?

- How are you going to be conscious of gender stereotypes or assumptions, from this moment or over the next few days?
- In which situations do you feel constrained to act in a particular way to safeguard their masculinity?

## A Prayer Ritual

### Preparation

○ Photocopy and distribute Handout 4-A, "Male and Female, God Created Them," one copy per person. You will need one large candle and eight smaller candles about the size of vigil lights.

**1.** Divide the group into two halves, Side One and Side Two, and have them sit facing each other.

**2.** Place one large candle and eight smaller candles in the center of the group. Ask for eight volunteers each to light a smaller candle at the end of each response.

**3.** Begin with silence for one minute. Light the larger candle in the center of the group as the leader recites the first part of the prayer. Recite the rest of the prayer pausing and lighting a smaller candle after each verse.

**4.** Conclude with the Lord's Prayer and a sign of peace.

## Expressions of Sexuality

The activities in the first section focused on the dimensions of sexuality that included our identity as a gendered person and the expression of our sexuality in relationship to ourselves, others and God. This section will become more specific about expressing our sexuality in relationship with others.

### Additional Activity: Media Messages

### Preparation

○ Bring in a number of magazines (ask the boys to bring any from home). Include weekly news magazines; men's magazines like *Esquire, Details, GQ,* and *Maxim;* and fitness magazines aimed at men like *Men's Health* and *Men's Fitness.*

**1.** Divide the boys into pairs with the following instructions:
Scan the magazines and newspapers. Pay particular attention to the way the media portrays the sexuality of men. Take about fifteen minutes to discuss with your partner the following questions:
- What are the dominant messages of how sexuality is portrayed?
- Are they life giving in the sense that they will encourage people to live in wholeness? Are they affirming of sacred human dignity?

- How realistic are these images for the typical male?
- Why does the media portray these messages as they do? Whose interests drive media messages?

Select several pictures from the magazines to illustrate your answers.

**2.** In the large group, invite the pairs to report their observations or insights. Ask the group to offer further examples of media messages from movies, television, music, and other forms of advertising.

**3.** In your own words, sum up the observations of the group. Discuss how it is likely that the dominant message in the media is that "if you really love someone, then you show it by sleeping with them."

**4.** Read aloud the following extract from *Matthew, Mark, Luke & You* by William J. O'Malley:

> I was a breech birth, which means I came into the world folded in half, not headfirst but rear-end first. As a result, my mother was so torn by the delivery she had to have a great many stitches. The doctor told my father he should stay out of bed with her for about three months. But my father, the kindest man, didn't want to take the slightest risk of causing her even the slightest pain. So he stayed out of bed with her for a year. (pp. 50–51)

**5.** Ask the group to reflect on this story. Read it again and this time continue with: O'Malley then asks, "Which way did he show more love for her—by getting into bed with her, or by staying out of bed? Is it possible there's an even greater way of showing love than sex?"

**6.** Ask group members to journal their responses to O'Malley's story.
- What is O'Malley saying? What is his point? Does it convey a truth often missed by popular secular culture?
- Is this a different message compared to the dominant media messages?

### Activity: What the Church Says!
People often speak with great authority on "what the Church says" about human sexuality, and they are often quite wrong. Misinformation complicates the topic of sexuality. It is important to know what the Church really does say and also to have some understanding of what those statements mean.

#### Preparation
○ Make one copy of Handout 4-B, "What the Church Says About Sexuality," for each member of the group plus extra copies for cutting in small groups of three to five boys each. Provide one large sheet of newsprint, paper, scissors and glue for each group.

**1.** Gather the group into a circle. Introduce the activity in your own words as follows:

Often when in an argument, people will say things like, "Everyone says that . . .", "All my friend parents say . . .", or "They say that . . .". Have you every wondered who the "they" in "they said" really is? Likewise, when people say "the Church says . . .", the Church often gets misquoted. Myths about "what the Church says . . ." grow to take on the credibility of fact, regardless of the truth they contain. This is often the case when people discuss sex and human sexuality. It is important to know what the Church really does say. Since Church teaching is rooted in Scripture, let's begin with a look at the prophet Micah. Micah tells us what God requires of us: act justly, love tenderly and walk humbly with our God (adapted from Mic. 6:8).

**2.** Divide the group into small groups of three to five. Give each group a large piece of newsprint, individual copies of Handout 4-B, "What the Church Teaches About Sexuality," one extra copy of the handout, scissors, and glue. On the board or on posted newsprint, draw three large intersecting circles. Have one person in each group duplicate the drawing, taking up as much of the newsprint as they can.

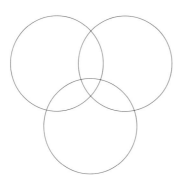

Label the three circles with the three statements from Micah.

**3.** "What does it mean to 'act justly, love tenderly, walk humbly' with respect to sexuality? Brainstorm possibilities with the group for about ten minutes.

**4.** Tell the groups to look at the handout "What the Church Teaches About Sexuality." Discuss how each of the statements applies to one or more of the three statements from Micah. Cut each statement and glue it on or near the circle that is most compatible with the statement, or place the statement in one of the intersecting spaces. Demonstrate for the large group by taking one statement, discussing how it applies, and gluing it in the appropriate place on the posted newsprint. Allow the group fifteen to twenty minutes to complete the task.

**5.** Have each group show and explain to the rest what they have processed. Sum up the findings of the group, emphasizing the positive nature of the Church's approach to human sexuality.

**6.** Allow five to ten minutes for journaling using the following questions:
- What is surprising to you about the Church's teaching on sexuality?
- What direction does the Church give you in living as a sexual male?
- What questions or issues of sexuality do you still wrestle with?

## Additional Activity: Words of Love

### Preparation
○ Photocopies of Handout 4-C: "Words of Love," one for each group member.

**1.** Gather group into a circle and sit for a moment in silence to settle and focus attention of the group. Select a reflection from the sheet and ask a volunteer to read it aloud. Pause for a moment then ask a second reader to reread it so that the perspective of a different voice may open further insights.

**2.** Ask the group to journal for five to ten minutes their response, reaction, or insights into the verse.

**3.** Instruct the group to gather into threes and take turns listening to each other as they talk about where that verse has led them. Each person has four minutes in which to speak. During this time, the role of the other group members is to listen. They cannot speak or ask questions. After four minutes, they have two minutes to ask clarifying questions of the speaker. (Question time is not a time for comment.)

**4.** After fifteen minutes, regather the group and invite them to share insights, reactions, responses, and new questions that that have emerged.

## Activity: Rules for Authentic Sexuality
There is not much point in talking and thinking about sexuality unless the individuals present are encouraged to internalize the wisdom arising from these activities.

**1.** Gather the group into a circle and distribute Handout 4-D, "Rules for Authentic Sexuality," a list of guidelines for living the sacredness of sexuality.

**2.** Discuss each one asking group members to explain what each rule means to them.

**3.** Invite group members to spend 10–15 minutes journaling their own rules for their sexuality of authentic manhood.

# Resource Materials

## Internet

*www.theologyofthebody.net* is the online resource for Pope John Paul II's "Theology of the Body." As well as articles from official Church documents, it also has a listing of conferences and events around the world, online discussion, resource materials, details of local study groups, and links to other Web sites.

## Print Materials

Bartlett, Bob. *Growing Toward Intimacy: Helping Catholic Teens Integrate Spirituality and Sexuality.* Saint Paul, MN: Good Ground Press, 2002. An excellent read for adolescents, this book is engaging and forthright, honest and humorous. Bartlett's approach, which places sexuality and sex in the context of relationships, is a healthy take on the Church's teachings on sexuality.

Bausch, William J. *Becoming a Man: Basic Information, Guidance and Attitudes on Sex for Boys.* Mystic, CT: Twenty-Third Publications, 1988. This book for boys, and those who teach, live, or work with them, is packed with information that covers topics from sexuality and relationships to masturbation, pornography, and homosexuality.

Claussen, Janet, with Keller, Ann. *Seeking: Doing Theology with Girls.* Winona, MN: Saint Mary's Press, 2003. This manual has a chapter titled "A Theology of Sexuality" (pp. 111–134). Although written specifically for adolescent girls, this resource is useful because it also has application to adolescent boys in coming to awareness of themselves as both same and different. The "Sexual Integrity FAQ's" (pp. 130–131) would be useful in group discussion with boys.

Ferder F., & Heagle J. *Tender Fires: The Spiritual Promise of Sexuality.* New York: Crossroad, 2002. As Catholic religious educators and counselors, the authors draw on their pastoral experience with theological insight and the wisdom necessary to approach sexuality with authenticity. This is a book for adults interested in exploring a healthy theology of sexuality.

Sacred Congregation for Catholic Education. *Educational Guidance In Human Love.* Homebush, Australia: St. Paul Publications, 1984. These resources are official publications of the Catholic Church, and useful for reference in discerning the position and teaching of the Church.

Whitehead E. E., & Whitehead J. D. *Wisdom of the Body: Making Sense of Our Sexuality.* New York: Crossroad, 2001. The Whiteheads are recognized across the world as significant Catholic writers and educators. Their perspective as a married couple gives their treatment of sexuality a credibility and reality that can only come from a lived understanding of the sacrament of marriage.

# Male and Female, God Created Them

**Leader:** God, you created us male and female, in your image, you created all of us. Help us to live out our birthright gifts and so reflect your image and likeness in this world.

*Pause and light a candle*

**Side 1:** For every woman who is tired of acting weak when she knows that she is strong, there is a man who is tired of pretending to be strong when he feels vulnerable.

*Pause and light a candle*

**Side 2:** For every man who is burdened with the constant expectation of "knowing everything," there is a woman who is tired of acting dumb.

*Pause and light a candle*

**Side 1:** For every woman who is tired of being called an "emotional female," there is a man who is denied the right to weep and to be gentle.

*Pause and light a candle*

**Side 2:** For every man who must worry about [being macho], there is a woman who is tired of being treated like a sex object.

*Pause and light a candle*

**Side 1:** For every woman who feels "tied down" by her children, there is a man who is denied the full pleasures of shared parenthood.

*Pause and light a candle*

**Side 2:** For every man who must bear full financial responsibility for another human being, there is a woman who is denied meaningful employment or equal pay.

*Pause and light a candle*

**Side 1:** For every woman denied access to learning, there is a man who is denied the opportunity for being.

*Pause and light a candle*

**Side 2:** For every woman and man who are freed to be truly themselves, the image and likeness of God shines a little more brightly in our world.

*Pause and light a candle*

Adapted from Nancy R. Smith, "For Every Woman,"
in *Images of Women in Transition,* compiled by Janice Grana
(Winona, MN: Saint Mary's Press, 1991), p. 49.
Copyright 1976 by The Upper Room, Nashville, Tennessee.
Used with permission of Upper Room Books.

# "What the Church Says"

The Catechism of the Catholic Church says:

**#2332**  Sexuality affects all aspects of the human person in the unity of his body and soul.

**#2337**  Chastity means the successful integration of sexuality within the person and thus the inner unity of man in his bodily and spiritual being. Sexuality, in which man's belonging to the bodily and biological world is expressed, becomes personal and truly human when it is integrated into the relationship of one person to another, in the complete and lifelong mutual gift of a man and a woman.

**#2342**  Self-mastery is a *long and exacting work*. One can never consider it acquired once and for all. It presupposes renewed effort at all stages of life. The effort required can be more intense in certain periods, such as when the personality is being formed during childhood and adolescence.

**#2347**  The virtue of chastity blossoms in *friendship*. . . . Chastity is expressed notably in *friendship with one's neighbor*. Whether it develops between persons of the same or opposite sex, friendship represents a great good for all. It leads to spiritual communion.

**#2354**  *Pornography* consists in removing real or simulated sexual acts from the intimacy of the partners, in order to display them deliberately to third parties. . . . It does grave injury to the dignity of its participants (actors, vendors, the public), since each one becomes an object of base pleasure and illicit profit for others.

**#2362**  Sexuality is a source of joy and pleasure: "The Creator himself . . . established that in the [generative] function, spouses should experience pleasure and enjoyment of body and spirit. . . ." (Pope Pius XII, Discourse, October 29, 1951).

The Sacred Congregation for Catholic Education says:

**#5**  Sexuality characterizes man and woman not only on the physical level, but also on the psychological and spiritual, making its mark on each of their expressions. Such diversity, linked to complementarity of the two sexes, allows thorough response to the design of God according to the vocation to which each one is called. . . .

**#6**  Sexuality, oriented, elevated and integrated by love acquires truly human quality. . . .

**#22**  In the Christian vision of man and woman, a particular function of the body is recognized, because it contributes to the revealing of the meaning of life and of the human vocation.

Adapted from *Educational Guidance in Human Love:
Outlines for Sex Education*
(Homebush, Australia: St. Paul Publications), pp. 9–10, 19–20.

The quote from Pope Pius XII is from the English translation of the *Catechism of the Catholic Church* for use in the United States of America (*CCC*), numbers 2332, 2337, 2342, 2347, 2354, and 2362. Copyright © 1994 by the United States Catholic Conference, Inc.—Libreria Editrice Vaticana. Used with permission.

# Words of Love

## "Restless Love"

God of all heaven and earth,
St. John reminded us that you are Love,
Love Eternal,
Love forever new and exciting,
Love endlessly giving.
It is little wonder our lives are restless.

Guide me so that I may find my way
To rest in You
To rest in Love

## "Awareness of Love"

Yahweh,
You revealed yourself to us as, I AM
So that I may know you in awareness.
Blessed be the experiences of falling in love
That make me aware of sun shining, birds singing
and music playing.
Blessed is being in love
That makes me feel excited to be alive
Feel the butterflies in my stomach
Long to see my love
To hear her voice
To be bathed in her laugh
To feel her embrace.
Blessed are these moments of awareness
For they point me to You
Stirring my heart
Waiting for me to know that You Are.

## "Body, Soul & Spirit"

Source of all Love
Love Itself,
Longing of my longing
Desire of my desires,
In Your infinite wisdom
You made me in Your likeness and image
So that I may know love and know You
In the sensations and stirrings of my body
The Temple of the Spirit,
So that my Soul may recognize its source in
The richness of
The Source of all Love.

## "The Name of God is Love"

Restless, erotic fire of passion
Making me aware of my heart beating with
	excitement,
Opening me to the possibility of richness and
	blessing,
Daring to dream and hope
Somehow believing,
Not knowing, yet,
Knowing that I am not alone.
Believing that love is life giving
but fearing my broken heart that
I know too well makes me feel like I am dying
Because of promise unspoken
Help me trust that
"Nothing is impossible for God"
whose name is Love.

# Rules for Authentic Sexuality

- Acknowledge that God is always present and ask honestly if your actions honor God's gift of sexuality.
- Sexual activity means commitment. Let's not pretend we are ready to commit when we are not.
- Sexual activity means vulnerability. We expose ourselves and others to great hurt, especially when a relationship ends. Loving men protect their partners from harm. Smart men do not set themselves up to be hurt.
- Sexual activity involves powerful passions. It takes time and self-discipline to learn to control them. It is a lie to say a young man can go only "so far" and then stop. Authentic men don't lie to themselves or their partners.
- Males and females may use the same words but they are most likely to be saying and hearing different things. Physically, emotionally, and psychologically ask honestly what the other is really yearning for. Men who are authentic don't manipulate others.
- Females admire and desire males who have a reputation for respecting females.
- Sexual urges cannot be ignored. Men learn to master their urges and this leads to happiness because they know happiness and short term pleasure is not the same thing.
- Pray over Jesus' words, "[B]y this everyone will know that you are my disciples, if you have love for one another" (John 13:35) and resolve to do the loving thing.

# A Retreat for Fathers and Sons

## Overview

My eldest son still sometimes speaks of the first weekend the two of us just dropped out together. He was experiencing "growing pains" and for most of the weekend I sat with him or we walked together saying very little as I felt the inadequacy of not finding the words to say something intelligent and productive. I felt like I had failed. I found this tough, especially after working for many years with adolescents like him. It turned out I was wrong. I came to realize I hadn't failed because in the following days and weeks, my wife kept saying, "I don't know what you said to that boy, but it worked."

The retreat program has come a long way and touched many fathers and sons since then. Although you will probably find the format of this retreat very different from your typical youth retreat, trust the process. It works because when sons experience their fathers squandering their time on them, they grow into fine young men.

What do fathers want? In most cases they want their sons to live happy, meaningful, and fruitful lives. They also want their sons to know how much their sons mean to them.

What do sons want? They want to know that their fathers are proud of them so that they feel as though they can stand with them, shoulder to shoulder, man to man.

What do fathers need? They need support and reassurance in their most important task of fathering. They also need to take time with their sons.

What do sons need? Their fathers need to squander time on them. If this happens, they grow up feeling supported and self-assured.

Sadly, fathers and sons simply spending time together is increasingly a rare occurrence. As a result, "father-hunger" or the "father-wound" remains the deepest yearning of too many males as they grow into manhood. Psychologists and social commentators, identify the father-hunger as perhaps one of the most significant social malaises of our time. It does not have to be this way. Each and every father, regardless of his circumstances, can make a difference to the lives of their sons, our society, and future generations—simply by "being there" for his son.

The father/son retreat constructs an opportunity for fathers to be there for their sons. During this time together, the retreat process will help fathers and sons engage in conversations of great importance. Hopefully, the conversations will continue throughout life. Yet many men are reluctant to take the opportunity afforded by a father/son retreat. To address this reluctance, it is important to first debunk some fallacies:

**Fallacy #1:** I am just an ordinary guy, nothing special. I have made a lot of mistakes fathering my son. I love him, but I haven't done a very good job. Retreats are for the "super-dads."

**Truth #1:** God knows best. God knows all of our limits, failings, and weaknesses. God chose you to be this boy's father. Out of all the males ever created, you were the only one with the exact balances of weakness and goodness required to raise this boy to be a son of God.

**Fallacy #2:** I couldn't get into all the "personal" stuff required. There are some things from my past I am not proud of and I don't ever want him to know them.

**Truth #2:** You only have to share what you wish to. Each time we tell our sons something like, "I just can't talk about that. I wish I could but I just can't bring myself to . . . ," we admit to our failings, which takes the pressure off our sons. They will not be subject to the tyranny that they have to be perfect.

**Fallacy #3:** Retreats like that are too emotional. I am not the emotional type (I leave that up to my wife).

**Truth #3:** Father/son retreats are not designed to be emotional. They are designed so that the sons do not have to enter the world of men alone, pretending. When people are honest about how much they mean to each other, feelings become transparent. Too many fathers die without their sons ever really knowing for sure if their father loved them.

**Fallacy #4:** Retreats are too religious. I am not the religious type.

**Truth #4:** Most of the events of our daily existence don't look like liturgy, prayerful silence, or prayerful language, but our lives are where God is present with us. That makes every moment of your life sacred.

## Planning a Retreat

There is no one right way for a father to retreat with his son. The design of this retreat suggests one process that has proven effective. When and where the retreat takes place is up to you. The variety of venues and formats are limited only by your imagination. The leader of this retreat should not try to be a participant at the retreat. Each father needs to have his sole attention on his son.

### The Venue

The venue can be a camping ground, church meeting room, family room, or any place that allows space, privacy, and the opportunity to move about. A venue with opportunities for walking or spending time in nature while keeping silence is most conducive to the flow of this retreat.

### The Group

A retreat can consist of one father and one son spending time together. Or a group of fathers may decide to spend the weekend together with their sons and their friends. A third alternative is to pick a date and advertise an invitation at the parish or school, for anyone else interested to join in. Each father and son pair is the focus for a father/son retreat, so it makes little difference if the participants know each other.

## The Format

The format is simply the vehicle or the opportunity to bring fathers and sons together in an environment that encourages much-needed conversation. This format for father/son retreat does not come out of a theory of youth ministry or psychology. It comes out of successful father/son retreat experiences. It involves stillness, reflection, and silence. Males often do not realize how they avoid these things until they try to practice them. We have an urge to fill every space with words or actions. Allowing the space to be free of words and actions teaches us something about communication, as well as the significance of words.

The basic format of this father/son retreat consists of five or six sessions, each lasting around one-and-a-half hours. Ideally, the sessions would run from dinner time on a Friday night until Saturday night, leaving open the option to spend the night with departure after breakfast Sunday morning:

| | |
|---|---|
| **Friday Evening** | Gather for a meal |
| | *Session One*—My boy/my dad: What a story! |
| | Watch a movie together (optional) |
| **Saturday** | Gather for breakfast |
| | *Session Two*—It 's not easy being a man. |
| | Morning Break |
| | *Session Three*—"You've gotta have friends . . ." |
| | Lunch |
| | *Session Four*—"What am I supposed to do with my life?" |
| | Afternoon Break |
| | *Session Five*—Saint Joseph and Jesus |
| | Free Time |
| | Dinner |
| | *Session Six*—Closing Liturgy |

Session Six can also take place on Sunday morning. Liturgy may be a Eucharistic liturgy or a prayer service. Adjust the schedule to fit the time and setting of your retreat.

Experience in running father/son retreats has shown that alternative successful formats might include weekly sessions of an hour and a half each, a couple of all day meetings or a combination of a half-day followed by several follow-up meetings.

## Preparation

○ Arrange discretely for wives/mothers and/or other family members to write letters of affirmation to retreat participants. Ensure that they will be delivered to you before the retreat, allowing time for follow-up and reminders so that every father and son will receive a letter. The letters will have the most significant impact on participants if the participants are unaware they are getting a letter from home.

- Look ahead to each session. Photocopy the questions or instructions that participants will need in their writing assignments. Note that some of the questions for fathers are different than the sons' questions. You may want to use half-sheets of paper for each. Also, using different color paper for each session will make them easier to reference. Consider posting them on newsprint for easy reference in the large group.

- For Session Four, write out the following in large print on separate pieces of poster board:
  - Scripture verses from step 1
  - Plato quotation from step 2

- Look ahead to the last session which includes a closing liturgy. Decide whether a Mass or Prayer Service is most appropriate for your group and setting. Arrange for a priest if the group will be celebrating Eucharistic liturgy. Brief him ahead of time about the retreat, and give him a copy of the theme and format so that he can incorporate it into the homily. Ask about the possibility of a shared homily among the participants and which readings you will be using. Whether you decide to celebrate Eucharist or a prayer service, refer to pages 37–42 in Part One of this manual for ideas about creating and enhancing rituals.

- Obtain the following supplies and resources for the retreat:
  - a large candle
  - matches
  - a Bible
  - blank notebooks (one for each individual participant)
  - a pen for each participant
  - CD/cassette player
  - copies of the following for each participant:
    - Handout 5-A, "Prayers for a Father/Son Retreat"
    - Handout 5-B, "My Vocation—My Calling"
    - one copy of Resource 5-A, "A Story of a Father and a Son"

**Videos**

- You will need a VCR and one of the following videos for Friday night's optional movie time. The following movies all deal with men learning to live lives to the full. They should be readily available at the local video store except for *All Men Are Sons* (see order information to obtain this video).
  - *Tuesdays with Morrie* (Harpo Films, 1999), runs for 89 minutes. This movie tells the story of a young man learning about what really matters from an old man. This movie explores many of the issues of being a man and the value of a life richly lived.
  - *October Sky* (Universal, 1999) runs for 108 minutes. This movie tells the story of a high school boy called Homer as he strives to fulfill his dreams. As he matures, so does his relationship with his father.
  - *Mr. Holland's Opus* (Hollywood Pictures, 1995) tells the story of a man's life experiences as he finds meaning and purpose in the discovery of his vocation, which was not what he thought it was in the beginning of the movie. Along the

way, his relationships with his wife, son, and colleagues all evolve and help make him the man he was born to be.

- *All Men Are Sons* (John Badalament and Chad Grochowski, 2002). This documentary, screened on PBS, captures a range of father/son relationships in their complexity and simplicity through the unfolding stories of a group of men reflecting on their own father/son relationships. More information, including ordering details, is available at the Web site *www.allmenaresons.com/film/film.html.*

### Music

○ The success of Session One depends on the two songs below. Obtain recordings of these songs.

- "Beautiful Boy" by John Lennon (1980), found on *Imagine: Music from the Motion Picture,* Capitol Records, 1988.
- "The Old Man" by Phil Coulter, found on *The Live Experience* by Phil Coulter and His Orchestra, Four Seasons Music, 1995.

○ In addition, bring a collection of quiet, instrumental music; for example, "Sacred Treasures—Choral Masterworks from Russia" (1990, San Francisco: Hearts of Space)

○ Also, see the suggested musical resources in the Introduction to this manual.

## Session One: My Boy/My Dad—What a Story!

If the retreat takes place over a weekend, consider beginning with an evening meal on Friday night for the participants. Whenever you begin, allow time for welcoming the participants, so that they can become familiar with the retreat venue. If the group is large and unfamiliar to each other, use name tags. Allow time for the men to mix informally and introduce themselves to one another.

**Note:** Throughout the retreat, use the word "men," not "men and boys," whenever possible.

**1.** Welcome the participants to the retreat. To establish the climate for the retreat, have them gather in a circle with each man standing next to his son. Light the large candle. Invite them to be seated.

**2.** Read or say in your own words the following script:

❧ It is important to be mindful of what a retreat is. A retreat is quality time together. The Scriptures are full of examples of men in retreat. Abraham, Moses, and the prophets also found retreat time essential to their becoming the men God destined them to be. Perhaps the most famous is Jesus' Wilderness retreat after his baptism (Luke 4:1–11). Interestingly, Jesus spent many significant moments alone with the Father and this was often recorded as time on the mountain.

♪ Taking the lead from these most significant figures in our tradition, we come away together in retreat. We withdraw from all that demands our attention and retreat into a sacred time and sacred space, the holy ground of the relationship between fathers and sons. As Jesus said, "the kingdom of God is among you" (Luke 17:21). When we come together, we turn off our mobile phones and consciously disconnect from whatever else governs our daily lives. In this way we retreat from all the distractions of the world and give ourselves, the greatest gift we have, to each other. In doing this we discover the richness we receive in giving.

Every session of this retreat is different. Coming to each session without expectations is an advantage. Trust the process to lead you where you are ready to be led. Once we cover something, we will move on, acknowledging that there is probably more to be done. This is an invitation for each father and son not to leave their experience at the retreat, but take it into the coming days, weeks, and months together.

**3.** Distribute prayer sheets, books, and pens to each participant. Select and read one of the prayers from Handout 5-A, "Prayers for a Father/Son Retreat."

**4.** Give the following explanation:
♪ One of the most central features of this retreat is the opportunity for fathers and sons to converse with each other through a simple procedure. This procedure or process involves the following steps:
   ○ The first step is to write down your thoughts about a particular "stimulus." In this case, it is the song we just heard. But it could also be a reading, a talk, or a memory of something from your past.
   ○ Next, you will swap books with each other and read what the other has written. The time spent reading the writing of the other is invaluable. It gives the other a chance to say all he can without the interruption that naturally occurs as part of everyday conversation. It is important to read slowly with all your attention and without interrupting each other. Then reread.
   ○ Take turns asking questions and clarifying what the other has written. Often fathers and sons both feel like the other "never listens" to what he says. The point of these conversations is not necessarily to achieve consensus. The point is to let both participants see that the other has heard them and acknowledges them. Asking clarifying questions is evidence of the gift of listening.
   ○ Be prepared to sit for times in silence together. Silence does not have to always be interrupted with words. When a father and son become comfortable with just being together, the connection between them is enriched in a way that is far beyond words.

As facilitator, you will need to check that at least one member of each father/son pair has a watch to keep time. If not, you can walk amongst the groups keeping time for them by giving a time call or ringing a bell.

## Activity: The Old Man

1. Read or say in your own words, the following introduction:

𝄕 Spiritual transformation is at the heart of the transition of a male from boyhood into manhood. Often we don't recognize the most profoundly sacred moments in a man's life as religious moments, because they happen outside our experience of going to church. But God is present with us in our daily experiences of life "where the rubber meets the road."

**2.** Play the song "The Old Man" by Phil Coulter on the CD player, asking participants to listen closely to the lyrics.

**3.** Tell the group that they will now practice the simple conversation procedure described earlier. Ask fathers and sons to reflect on the lyrics of the song they just heard by considering these questions (**Note:** read and post the questions. Also, distribute copies of the questions and the subsequent instructions):
- What does this song have to say about your relationship with your own father?
- What does the song have to say about your own father/son relationship?
Tell the participants to write about a page on each of the questions. Allow about ten to fifteen minutes. Replay the song at least once as they are writing.

**4.** Invite the participant pairs to find their own space away from the others somewhere in the vicinity. They need privacy to read what each other has to say and to have the first conversation. Read and post the following instructions:
- Take about ten minutes to read what the other has written. The reading will take less than ten minutes but go ahead and reread the material. Use the full 10 minutes to demonstrate that you are genuinely interested in what the other says.
- Taking turns, spend 15 minutes asking any clarifying questions of each other.
- The group will regather back here in 40 minutes.
Post the time.

**6.** Give group members a couple of minutes notice of the regathering time and invite them to start rejoining the group. Remember to give a two-minute warning any time you want to regather the group.

**7.** Allow five minutes for any discussion of the activity. Remind the group that this is the first session. We will continue to discuss many issues together as the sessions unfold.

## Activity: Beautiful Boy

**1.** Tell the group to pay close attention to the lyrics of "Beautiful Boy" by John Lennon as you play the song.

**2.** Ask each person to write for ten minutes about how they react and respond to the song. Use these questions as a way to get started.

- Questions for the father: What does this song have to say to you now that your son is no longer a little boy? What memories does it stir?
- Questions for the son: How do you react to this song? How do you see your father in comparison to the way you did when you were a boy. What does this song say about you and your dad?

**3.** Again ask the fathers and sons to find their own private space in pairs. Swap books and read for five minutes and then spend ten minutes taking turns asking clarifying questions of the other. Reiterate that the group will regather together in thirty minutes. Set and post the time.

**4.** Regather the group. Encourage discussion of insights or awareness that may have occurred during the conversations. Allow about five to ten minutes for the discussion.

**5.** Invite all present to come to prayer together by focusing on the candle and taking a moment of silence. Invite those present to pray aloud as they feel comfortable to do so. Begin by asking God to bless the relationships between all the men in the room. Select a prayer from the prayer sheet and invite the group to pray it aloud together.

**6.** Officially acknowledge the end of Session One and confirm the time and place of gathering for next session.

## Optional Activity: Movie Time

**1.** Show one of the movies recommended in the introduction to this retreat.

**2.** Following the movie, tell each father and son to check in with each other. Give them a question or two to ponder and discuss, like:
If this movie was a parable, what is it saying to you? It may have one message for a father and another message for a son. There is no need to analyze the movie; simply observe and share what it says to you.

**Note:** You may find additional questions for the movie *October Sky* on page 69 in the chapter "Power in the Hearts of Men." For the film *Tuesdays with Morrie,* check out the questions on page 55 in chapter "Who Am I (Becoming)?" Consider duplicating the questions and leading a group discussion with fathers and sons who want this option.

## Session Two: It's Not Easy Being a Man

**1.** Gather and welcome everyone back. Begin with a moment of silence. Light a candle and invite participants to say together one of the prayers from the prayer sheet.

**2.** Spend a brief moment or two checking in with each other to see if there are any afterthoughts from Session One.

**3.** Read aloud Resource 5-A, "A Story of a Father and a Son" by Robert Fulghum.

**4.** In your own words, comment on how this is a good story because it tells it like it is. Make a brief connection with the father and son in the story of the prodigal son (Luke 15:11–32). The story of the prodigal son doesn't sound like a particularly religious or holy story. Still, there were probably many men who could relate to this story when Jesus told it. Maybe Jesus was trying to let the men around him know that the stories of their struggles point us toward an understanding of God in relationship with us. This makes our stories every bit as sacred as this well-loved parable from Scripture. It is just sometimes we fail to recognize them as such.

**5.** Remind the group of the procedure they will follow:
♪ First, spend thirty minutes writing your responses to the questions. Second, swap notebooks and spend ten to fifteen minutes reading what the other has written. Third, take turns asking clarifying questions for thirty minutes. You will have a total of seventy-five minutes together.
Post the time when the group will come back together.

**6.** Hand out individual copies of the appropriate questions to fathers and sons.
- Questions for the father:
  - Write about your experience of finding out you were going to be a father. Remember your anticipation, excitement and apprehensions.
  - Recall the birth of your son and remember what it was like and how you felt. Were you present at the delivery? How did you feel about being there or not being present? What was it like to have your new son home from the hospital?
  - What are your favorite memories of the times between your son's birth and this moment?
  
  **Note:** If your son is adopted, change these questions as appropriate.
- Questions for the son:
  - Write about your first memories of your father.
  - In what ways do you want to be like him when you are a father?
  - What are you most grateful for when you think of your life with your father up to this point?
  - Imagine yourself and your father doing things together in ten years' time. How do you want to see the relationship between the two of you?

**7.** Regather the group and allow a few moments to share their reflections.

**8.** Pray together one of the prayers from the prayer sheet.

**9.** Formally end the session, again reminding the group members that there is much more that could be discussed after this session. Encourage them to continue this discussion over the coming days and weeks. Set the time for the next session.

## Session Three: "You've Gotta Have Friends . . ."

**1.** Gather the group in a circle and begin with a moment of silence. Light a candle and begin with a prayer from the prayer sheet.

**2.** Have someone read the story of Saul's son Jonathan speaking with his father on behalf of David, whom Saul was planning to kill (1 Samuel 19:1–7).

**3.** Read aloud the following:

As we grow, we go through various stages. At the first stage of our lives we cling to our mothers for nurture, support and protection. Even when we grow too big to be carried, we still cling to our mothers emotionally and spiritually. This is normal and natural.

Psychologists have acknowledged that we tend to come to know the father as someone who leaves and enters the world of the home, and so the father is the first "other" we come to know. As we begin school, we come to know even more "others," and we learn, through experiences, that we like some of these others more than the rest and so we make our first friends.

When we reach adolescence, we shift gears psychologically in preparation for adulthood. At this time, we now no longer define our identity using our family as our sole reference point. Our friends—the people most like us in age and daily experience of life—become more significant in our awareness of our emerging identity. Put simply, we know who we are by the company we keep and the influence they have over us.

This does not mean that our families lose their influence over us. This is so deeply rooted within us, it lasts a lifetime. When we begin to become our unique selves, we search for others with whom we can identify. To fail to see this is to miss the importance of friends in our lives.

The other significant thing about friends is that it is with them, we learn the necessary skills of intimacy or self-sharing. This is necessary because as God recognized from the very beginning, it is not good for us to be alone (Gen. 2:18). The images of cool, distant men of television and the movies—men like the Lone Ranger, Batman, or characters typically played by John Wayne, Humphrey Bogart, and Arnold Schwarzenegger—usually don't have the skills for lasting relationships, making them poor role models for men.

Every experience of friendship helps us find our "true selves." Also, every experience of friendship prepares us for the most important relationships of our lives. Christianity has from the very beginning been centered on relationships. Unfortunately, the conditioning of males in our culture has not prepared us well for relationships. Believing that males need to be independent, competitive, and in control, many males enter adulthood unprepared for their most important relationships. For most men, their most important relationships will be that of husband and father.

**4.** Ask the group to ponder the term "circle of friends." We tend to think of people as either being inside or outside our circle of friends. Instruct the fathers and sons to each draw a full-page circle in their notebooks. Ask them to think of who their friends are, listing them accordingly. Those who are casual friends can be listed near the edge of the circle. Their very best friend can be listed at the center of the circle, and the others can be placed on a continuum between the center and the edge of the circle.

**5.** Ask the fathers and sons to consider where they would place each other in the circle and where they would like to have each other placed in the circle. Explain that this gives the participants permission to acknowledge that they may or may not have the desired level of intimacy with each other, allowing them to construct a goal of where they would like their relationships to go. Our relationships sometimes are not perfect, but if we want them to be better, we begin to make them better by acknowledging what it is that we would like to work toward.

**6.** Send the fathers and sons off with the following instructions. State that the group will come back together in an hour. Post the time.
Hand out these instructions:
- Spend a few minutes completing your individual circle of friends.
- Exchange notebooks and take another five minutes viewing each others' circle of friends.
- Sons, spend fifteen minutes explaining to your fathers the qualities of your friends. What makes them friends?
- Fathers, spend fifteen minutes telling your sons your most significant experiences of friendship. Do you have a lifelong friend? Who were your friends when you were your son's age? What is your most significant disappointment in a friendship?
- Spend about fifteen minutes asking clarifying questions about each others' friendships.

**7.** Regather the group into a circle. Ask the reassembled group to raise any issues or observations from their discussions they would like to share with the whole group. Ask the fathers if anyone would like to comment on a good friend that they don't get a chance to see very often.

**8.** Ask both fathers and sons to each imagine that their best friends from high school just walked in to this room. Have them respond in their notebooks to these questions:

- How would you react?
- What do you think that your best friend from high school would have to say to your son/father about you?

Take no more than ten minutes for this exercise. Invite the fathers and sons to find time during the coming days to come back to think about these questions, to write something and share it with each other. Ask them to set a date and place to do this at this time.

9. Ask for a volunteer to choose a prayer from the prayer sheet to pray together. Bring a formal close to the session, reminding the participants that this is one for them to come back to in the coming days.

## Session Four: "What Am I Supposed to Do With My Life?"

**1.** Gather in the circle in silence for a moment. Light a candle. Have someone read aloud from the Bible the story of the creation of man and the role God gives him (Gen. 2: 7–8, 15).

**2.** Display the poster board with a paraphrase of a quote attributed to the Greek philosopher Plato *(The Holy Longing)*. Have another person read it aloud as everyone ponders the words:

- "We are fired into life with a madness that comes from the gods
  and which would have us believe that we can have great love,
  perpetuate our own seed, and contemplate the divine." (p. 1)

**3.** Display the prepared poster board with the Scripture verse, drawing attention back to the Scripture that was included in the opening prayer. Ask the participants to consider the two quotes together for a moment and then, in their pairs, spend a brief moment talking about what they see as the connection between the two.

**4.** In the large group, spend about five to ten minutes drawing out some of the insights about the quotes from the father/son pairs.

**5.** Ask the participants to consider the following and to take notes in their note-books any points they wish to discuss with each other:

- Psychologists see the role of the father as significant in initiating their sons into the world of work. Work is very significant to the identity of men. It is no coincidence that the Scripture from the opening prayer tells us that, as soon as God created Adam, he put him to work in the garden. There is something work-oriented about the male psyche in that our identity is constructed not just by our family and peer group, but also from what we do. Theologically, the passage from Genesis is interpreted to mean that we are in the world to be cocreators with God.

In response to the question, "Tell me about yourself?", most men would respond, "I am a mechanic, doctor, teacher, clerk . . ." What we do is important to our sense of self and our relationship with God. But as with other things in life, a question of balance is essential for our well-being and wholeness. When men define themselves exclusively by their work, it dominates their life. When this happens, relationships suffer and ultimately their work impoverishes rather than enriches them. As a culture there are three significant problems with this out-of-proportion approach to work in our lives:

- The belief that our job, not our true selves, is central to what we are. This has significant consequences to men who lose their jobs. It also has significant impact on the authenticity of a man's relationships. In an age where the average man is expected to have at least four separate career paths in his lifetime, a man's sense of self and his relationships cannot depend on his job alone.
- In neglecting our obligation to keep the Sabbath, we lose our connection with reality by failing to take time to turn towards our Creator and be renewed and renourished. The consequences of this neglect are all around us—in lives that are constantly over-stressed and oriented toward life-defeating, rather than life-giving, goals and values. If we do not stop for Sabbath time, we might never hear God calling us to where we are meant to be in life.

**6.** Distribute the copies of the father and son questions:

- Questions for the father:
  - What does my work give me?
  - Would I work if financially I didn't have to? Explain.
  - What are my best experiences from work?
  - What do I wish someone had made me see about work, when I was my son's age?
  - If I could do it all again, what changes would I make to my approach to work?
- Questions for the son:
  - What sort of job do I want? (E.g., technology centered, people centered, office job, outdoors job, etc.)
  - Remembering back to my earliest childhood memories, what did I enjoy doing with my time? What bought me pleasure and what did I avoid?
  - What activity do I really enjoy doing? What do I always find that I have the energy for?
  - What is success and failure and how will I know them?

**7.** Distribute Handout 5-B: "My Vocation—My Calling." Give the following instructions:

♩ Spend ten to fifteen minutes reflecting on the passages. Using the passages as further stimulus for writing, answer the father or son questions in writing.
- ○ Swap books and read for ten minutes.
- ○ Spend about twenty minutes taking turns asking clarifying questions, talking, and listening.
- ○ This activity should be completed in about 60 minutes.

Post a time to regather as a whole group.

**8.** Regather the participants. Ask how any of the passages on the handout spoke to individuals. Select participants to read from the handout sheet as a final prayer.

## Session Five: Saint Joseph and Jesus

**1.** Gather the group in a circle for a moment of silence. Light the candle and read these passages about Joseph in the Gospel of Matthew (1:18–21 and 2:13–15). Ask the group to sit quietly for a moment and ponder the Scriptures.

**2.** Ask if anyone has any thoughts on the reading from Matthew's Gospel. Refer to Joseph's dream. Rhetorically ask if there was ever a father who didn't have dreams for his son. Read or tell the following in your own words:

♩ Do you ever wonder about what type of father Joseph must have been to raise a boy like Jesus? Wonder about how Joseph must have looked at his son as he first crawled, walked, and talked.

Imagine what it must have been like to live under what we consider "Third World" conditions in a land brutally ruled by a foreign army. What type of man must Joseph have been to ensure that Jesus didn't grow up full of anger and hatred like so many terrorist or freedom fighters we are familiar with in our world today? Where did Jesus learn how to treat women, the poor, and people in general, if not from his father Joseph?

We know very little of Joseph. He is only mentioned in a few lines of Scripture. However, if we think about the significance of the father/son relationship, we get an increasingly clearer picture of what Joseph must have been like. What led Jesus to think of God so affectionately as "Abba" or "Father"? This way of thinking was quite radical in Jesus' time. Where and how might the seeds of these thoughts been planted in Jesus?

**3.** Distribute copies of the following questions:
- Questions for the father:
  - ○ When you look at your son what do you admire?
  - ○ What are your son's gifts and talents?
  - ○ Our culture values "success" by achievement. Where do you see success that your son might or might not be aware of?
  - ○ What wisdom about the true nature of success (that you may have learned the hard way) do you want to pass on to your son?

- What are your dreams for your son? Why do you dream these particular dreams?
- What do you see as the best moments in life in which you want to be standing man to man with your son?
- What do you want to say to your son that you never want him to forget?

- Questions for the son:
  - When have you felt closest to your father?
  - When have you felt that you had his approval?
  - In what areas do you want him to acknowledge his approval of you?
  - In what areas do you long to feel like a man, man to man with your father?
  - What do you value and appreciate most about your father?
  - What have you learned or remembered about your father during this retreat?
  - What is the one thing that is most important to say to your father?

**4.** Remind the participants of the procedure:
- Spend twenty minutes writing your responses to the questions.
- Swap books and spend fifteen minutes reading.
- Take turns and spend twenty minutes each in listening, asking clarifying questions in dialogue.

This activity will take about one hour. Post the time to regather the group.

**5.** Call the participants back together in the circle and say the following in your own words:

> Many men have never heard their father's approval aloud. They know that their fathers loved them but they have never heard it said. Hearing the approval of the father, actually hearing them say they love us, is known as the father's blessing. Some experts suggest that it is the single most significant thing in a man's life.

**6.** Read aloud the verse from the account of the Transfiguration (Matthew 17:5). Reread this Scripture and ask the group what they heard. Share the following observations:

> Two things happened in this short verse. First, Jesus heard his Father's voice approving of him. Second, his friends also heard it. They knew at that moment, more than ever, that Jesus had something to say.

Too often, fathers go to their graves without ever telling their sons aloud of their approval. They assume that their sons know it so they don't have to say it. This Scripture reminds us that hearing this out loud was a significant moment, even for Jesus.

**7.** Pray together this passage from the Scriptures having the fathers and sons stand and place their hands on their son's shoulders and saying together, "This is my son, my beloved. With him I am well pleased. Listen to him."

**8.** Conclude this session by saying together the Lord's Prayer.

## Session Six: Closing Liturgy

Plan the closing liturgy keeping in mind the participants and the experience they have had during the retreat. Use the ideas for creating sacred space and rituals in part 1, pages 37–42, to plan for your final session together. Whether the closing liturgy is a Mass or a prayer service, consider the following elements as you prepare:

- Dimmed lighting, placement of a crucifix, the large candle from the retreat, incense, objects of significance chosen by participants.
- Music used throughout the retreat or liturgical music appropriate to readings. If any fathers and sons are musicians, invite them to play.
- Opening Prayer from the Prayer Sheet
- Scripture readings. You may want to use the readings of the day, Scripture readings from the retreat, or other Scripture passages.
- Homily. Ask the celebrant about a shared homily in dialogue with the participants.
- Petitions. Prepare a few ahead of time. Ask the participants to add their own.
- Offertory. Include a basket or container for the letters from home.
- Communion Meditation. Reverently distribute the letters from home, allowing silent time for reading these.
- Close with a final blessing like the one that follows:

> May you recognize in your life the presence, power and light of your soul.
> May you realize that you are never alone
> that your soul in its brightness and belonging
> connects you intimately with the rhythm of the universe.
> May you have respect for your own individuality and difference.
> May you realize that the shape of your soul is unique,
> That you have a special destiny here
> that behind the façade of your life there is
> something beautiful, good and eternal happening.
> May you learn to see yourself with the same delight,
> pride and expectation with which God sees you in every moment.

Prayer "A Blessing of Solitude" is from
O'Donohue, John, *Anam Cara*. London: Bantam, 1997, p. 161.
All rights reserved. Permission applied for.

As we go, let us offer each other a sign of peace.

## Notes

Use this space to jot notes, ideas, reminders, and additional resources.

# Prayers for a Father/Son Retreat

## Prayer of an Unknown Confederate Soldier

I asked for strength that I might achieve,
I was made weak so that I might learn humbly to obey.
I asked for health that I might do greater things;
I was given infirmity so that I might do better things.
I asked for riches that I might be happy;
I was given poverty that I might be wise.
I asked for power that I might have the praise of men;
I was given weakness that I might know my need for God.
I asked for all things so that I might enjoy life;
I was given life so that I might enjoy all things.
I got nothing I had asked for,
but everything I had hoped for
Almost despite of myself, my unspoken prayers were answered;
I am, among all men, most richly blessed.

> Reprinted from *A Man's Guide to Prayer*,
> edited by Linus Mundy
> (New York: The Crossroad Publishing Company,
> 1998), pp. 36–37. Copyright © 1998 by Linus
> Mundy. All rights reserved. Permission applied for.

## A Man's Prayer

Blessed are you Lord our God and Father of all life,
You have given to us our gift of manhood.
Teach me to honor this gift
and the many good things that flow from it.
Remind me that strength and power
have value in our surrender to you.
Give me the courage so that like Jesus
I can surrender myself with abandon
into your extravagant love.

## Blessing of Purpose and Destiny

Blessed are you Lord our God,
who has given to each of us
a personal destiny and purpose in life.

We thank You, God of mysterious ways,
That You have a holy design for each of us
We rejoice, that we are, each of us, special to you,
That our names are written in the palm of Your hand
And our place in history, our purpose for existing,
Is known within Your heart since endless ages.
Blessed are You, Lord our God,
Who has given each of us
A personal destiny and purpose in life.
Amen.

> Adapted from *Prayers for the Domestic Church:
> A Handbook for Worship in the Home,*
> by Edward Hays
> (Easton, KS: Forest of Peace Books, 1979), p. 59.
> Copyright © 1979 by Edward M. Hays.
> Used with permission.

## Prayer for Change

God help us to change. To change ourselves and to change our world. To know the need for it. To deal with the pain of it. To feel the joy of it. To undertake the journey without understanding the destination. The art of gentle revolution. Amen.

> Adapted from Michael Leunig, *A Common Prayer*
> (North Blackburn, Australia: HarperCollins Dove,
> 1990). Copyright © 1990 by Michael Leunig.
> Used with permission.

## Psalm 127: 1, 3–5

Unless the Lord builds the house,
Those who build it labor in vain.
Unless the Lord guards the city,
The guard keeps watch in vain.
. . .
Sons are indeed a heritage from the Lord,
The fruit of the womb a reward.
Like arrows in the hand of a warrior
Are the son's of one's youth.
Happy is a man who has his quiver full of them. . . .

**Handout 5-A:** Permission to reproduce this handout for program use is granted.

# "A Story of a Father and a Son"

*This is 1963.*

From deep in the canyoned aisles of a supermarket comes what sounds like a small-scale bus wreck followed by an air raid. If you followed the running box-boy armed with mop and broom, you would come upon a young father, his three-year-old son, an upturned shopping cart, and a good part of the pickles shelf—all in a heap on the floor.

The child, who sits on a plastic bag of ripe tomatoes, is experiencing what might nicely be described as "significant fluid loss." Tears, mixed with mucus from a runny nose, mixed with blood from a small forehead abrasion, mixed with saliva drooling from a mouth that is wide open and making a noise that would drive a dog under a bed. The kid has also wet his pants and will likely throw up before this little tragedy reaches bottom. He has that "stand back, here it comes" look of a child in a pre-urp condition.

The small lake of pickle juice surrounding the child doesn't make rescue any easier for the supermarket 911 squad arriving on the scene.

The child is not hurt. And the father has had some experience with the uselessness of the stop-crying-or-I'll-smack-you syndrome and has remained amazingly quiet and still in the face of the catastrophe.

The father is calm because he is thinking about running away from home. Now. Just walking away, getting into the car, driving away somewhere down South, changing his name, getting a job as a paperboy or a cook in an all-night diner. Something—anything—that doesn't involve contact with three-year-olds.

Oh sure, someday he may find all this amusing, but in most private part of his heart he is sorry he has children, sorry he married, sorry he grew up, and, above all, sorry that this particular son cannot be traded in for a model that works. He will not and cannot say these things to anybody, ever, but they are there and they are not funny.

The box-boy and the manager and the accumulated spectators are terribly sympathetic and consoling. Later, the father sits in his car in the parking lot, holding the sobbing child in his arms until the child sleeps. He drives home and carries the child up to his crib and tucks him in. The father looks at the sleeping child for a long time. The father does not run away from home.

*This is 1976.*

Same man paces my living room, carelessly cursing and weeping by turns. In his hand is what's left of a letter that has been crumpled into a ball and then uncrumpled again several times. The letter is from his sixteen-year-old son *(same son)*. The pride of his father's eye—or was until today's mail.

The son says he hates him and never wants to see him again. The son is going to run away from home. Because of his terrible father. The son thinks the father is a failure as a parent. The son thinks the father is a jerk.

What the father thinks of the son right now is somewhat incoherent, but it isn't nice.

Outside the house it is a lovely day, the first day of spring. But inside the house it is more like Apocalypse Now, the first day of one man's next stage of fathering. The old gray ghost of Oedipus has just stomped through his life. Someday—some long day from now—he may laugh about even this. For the moment there is only anguish.

He really is a good man and a fine father. The evidence of that is overwhelming. And the son is quality goods as well. Just like the father, they say.

"Why did this happen to me?" the father shouts at the ceiling.

Well, he had a son. That's all it takes. And it doesn't do any good to explain about that right now. First you have to live through it. Wisdom comes later. Just have to stand there like a jackass in a hailstorm and take it.

*This is 1988.*

Same man and same son. The son is twenty-eight now, married, with his own three-year-old son, home, career, and all the rest. The father is fifty.

Three mornings a week I see them out jogging together around 6:00 a.m. As they cross a busy street,

I see the son look both ways, with a hand on his father's elbow to hold him back from the danger of oncoming cars, protecting him from harm. I hear them laughing as they run on up the hill into the morning. And when they sprint toward home, the son doesn't run ahead but runs alongside his father at his pace.

They love each other a lot. You can see it.

They are very care-full of each other—they have been through a lot together, but it's all right now.

One of their favorite stories is about once upon a time in a supermarket . . .

*This is Now*

And the story is always. It's been lived thousands of times, over thousands of years, and the literature is full of examples of tragic endings, including that of Oedipus. The sons leave, kick away and burn all bridges, never to be seen again. But sometimes (more often than not, I suspect) they come back in their own time and take their own fathers in their arms. That ending is an old one too. The father of the Prodigal Son could tell you.

# My Vocation—My Calling

To be nobody but yourself in a world that is doing its
   best, day and night,
to make you everybody else,
means to fight the hardest battle
which any human being can fight,
and never stop fighting.

e.e. cummings,
in *The Ethiopian Tattoo Shop,* by Edward Hays
(Leavenworth, KS: Forest of Peace Publishing, Inc.,
1983), p. 60. Copyright © 1983 by Edward M. Hays.
Used with permission.

O God
Help me
to believe
the truth about myself
no matter
how beautiful it is!

Macrina Wiederkehr,
in *Seasons of Your Heart: Prayers and Reflections,*
by Macrina Wiederkehr O.S.B.
(New York: HarperCollins*Publishers,* 1991), page 71.
Copyright © 1991 by Macrina Wiederkehr.
All rights reserved.
Used with permission
of HarperCollins*Publishers,* Inc.

## Father/Son Retreat Prayer Sheet

O Lord God,
I have no idea where I am going,
I do not see the road ahead of me,
I cannot know for certain where it will end.

Nor do I really know myself,
and the fact that I think
I am following Your will
Does not mean that I am actually doing so.
But I believe
that the desire to please You
Does in fact please You.
And I hope that I have that desire
In all that I am doing.
I hope that I will never do anything apart from that
desire to please You.
And I know that if I do this
You will lead me by the right road
Though I may know nothing about it.
Therefore I will trust You always
Though I may seem to be lost
and in the shadow of death.
I will not fear,
For You are ever with me,
And You will never leave me
To make my journey alone.

From Thomas Merton,
in *A Seven Day Journey with Thomas Merton,*
by Esther de Waal.
(Ann Arbor, MI: Servant Publications, 1992),
pp. 37–38. Copyright by Esther de Waal.
Permission applied for.

## Appendix

# Parallel Activities with Adolescent Girls

Saint Mary's Press has been on the forefront of bringing gender-specific resources designed to meet the unique needs of adolescent girls and boys. The Voices Series of six manuals, created to address the spirituality of adolescent girls, are similar in format to this manual, *Digging Deep: Fostering the Spirituality of Young Men.* These six manuals are:

> *Awakening: Challenging the Culture with Girls*
> *Retreats: Deepening the Spirituality of Girls*
> *Prayer: Celebrating and Reflecting with Girls*
> *Church Women: Probing History with Girls*
> *Biblical Women: Exploring Their Stories with Girls*
> *Seeking: Doing Theology with Girls*

Finding the occasion and setting for doing "just boys" or "just girls" ministry can be challenging. Most Catholic schools and parishes work with mixed gender groups of adolescents. How can they incorporate gender-specific activities within their classes and programs?

Many of the activities in the Voices manuals and in *Digging Deep: Fostering the Spirituality of Young Men* can be easily adapted to mixed groups by presenting the topic, breaking into single gender groups for discussion, and returning to the large group to gain perspectives of the opposite sex.

Another way to foster spirituality from a gender perspective is to plan concurrent sessions. Consider pairing up the following topics and activities from *Digging Deep: Fostering the Spirituality of Young Men* with activities from the Voices manuals:

- "Gender Qualities" on page 77 of *Digging Deep* with the activities "Male and Female, God Created Them," pp. 30–42 of *Awakening: Challenging the Culture with Girls.*
- "Images of God" on page 76 of *Digging Deep* with "God Beyond All Names", page 86 of *Prayer: Celebrating and Reflecting with Girls,* or any activities in the

**Appendix:** Permission to reproduce this appendix for program use is granted.

section "Examining Our Images of God," pp. 61–85 of *Seeking: Doing Theology with Girls.*

- "Media Messages" on page 79 of *Digging Deep* with any of the activities from the section, "Media Messages," pp. 61–74 of *Awakening: Challenging the Culture with Girls.*

- The activities in the section "Who Am I (Becoming)?" in *Digging Deep* with "Befriending Ourselves," p. 88 in *Seeking: Doing Theology with Girls* or "The Me I Am," p. 92 of *Awakening: Challenging the Culture with Girls.*

- The activities in the section, "Power in the Heart of Men" in *Digging Deep* with the activities in "Challenging the Culture of Violence," pp. 75–91 of *Awakening: Challenging the Culture with Girls.*

- Pair up the activity "Sibling Rivalry" on page 63 of *Digging Deep* with the stories of Sarah and Hagar, Rachel and Leah, and Mary and Martha found in the "Voices of Biblical Women" Appendix, pp. 99–114 of *Biblical Women: Exploring Their Stories with Girls.* More information and activities about these women are in the sections "Getting to Know the Matriarchs," pp. 29–30 and "Mary and Martha" (under the sections "Called by Jesus" and "Theologians in Their Own Right"), pp. 75–78, of *Biblical Women.*

- The activities in "Sacred Sexuality" on pages 73–87 of *Digging Deep,* especially "Defining Sex and Sexuality", "What the Church Says", and "Rules for Authentic Sexuality" with comparable activities in "A Theology of Sexuality," pp. 111–134 of *Seeking: Doing Theology with Girls,* especially "Commitments, Boundaries and Integrity"; and the Resource "Sexual Integrity FAQ's," p. 130 of the same book.

- The Father/Son Retreat in the Appendix of *Digging Deep* with "The Wisdom of Mothers and Daughters" on page 27 of *Retreats: Deepening the Spirituality of Girls.*

**Acknowledgments** *(continued from copyright page)*

The scriptural quotations contained herein are from the New Revised Standard version of the Bible, Catholic Edition (NRSV). Copyright © 1993 and 1989 by the Division of Christian Education of the National Council of the Churches of Christ in the United States of America. All rights reserved.

The scriptural quotations cited as "adapted from" are freely adapted and are not to be interpreted or used as official translations of the Bible.

The words of Vincent J. Donovan on page 9 are quoted from *Christianity Rediscovered: An Epistle from the Masai,* 25th Anniversary Edition (London: SCM Press, 1982; Orbis Books, 2003), page 22. Copyright © 1978 and 1982 by Vincent J. Donovan and SCM Press Ltd. Used with permission.

The words of Saint Augustine on page 11 and Handout 1-A are quoted from *Praying with Saint Augustine,* compiled by Valeria Boldoni, translated by Paula Clifford (London: Triangle, 1987), page 40. Translation and Introduction copyright © 1987 by The Society for Promoting Christian Knowledge.

The exercise on page 39 was adapted from *Uh-Oh* by Robert Fulghum (London: HarperCollins*Publishers,* 1991), pages 77–78. Copyright © 1991 by Robert Fulghum. All rights reserved. Used with permission of HarperCollins*Publishers* Ltd.

The quotation of Edward Hays on page 40 is taken from *Prayer Notes to a Friend* (Easton, KS: Forest of Peace Publishing, 2002), page 1.

The prayer "Prayer for Serenity" on Handout 1-A is by Reinhold Neibuhr, 1926.

The poem on Handout 1-A is from *The Prayer Tree* by Michael Leunig (North Blackburn, Australia: HarperCollins Dove, 1991). Copyright 1991 by Michael Leunig. Used with permission.

The prayer on Handout 1-A, "Lord Make Me an Instrument of Your Peace," is by Saint Francis of Assisi.

The words of Thomas Merton on page 45 are quoted from *Seeds of Contemplation,* by Thomas Merton (Norfolk, CT: New Directions, 1949), page 10. Copyright © 1949 by Our Lady of Gethsemani Monastery.

The words of Parker Palmer on page 45 are paraphrased and taken from *Let Your Life Speak: Listening for the Voice of Vocation* (San Francisco: Jossey-Bass, 2000), page 12. Copyright © 2000 by Jossey-Bass Inc., Publishers. All rights reserved.

The concepts of authenticity on pages 46 to 47 are paraphrased from *Method in Theology,* by Bernard J. F. Lonergan (Toronto: University of Toronto Press, 1999), page 121.

The quote on page 47 is taken from *Manhood: A Book About Setting Men Free,* by Steve Biddulph (Sydney, Australia: Finch Publishing, 1994), page 1. Copyright © 1994 by Steve Biddulph and Shaaron Biddulph.

The piece of dialogue from *Tuesdays with Morrie* on page 54 comes from Harpo Films, 1999.

The excerpt of a poem "September 1, 1939" on page 55 is taken from *Another Time,* by W. H. Auden (New York: Random House, 1940). Copyright © 1949 by W. H. Auden, renewed by the Estate of W. H. Auden.

The poem "Who Am I?" by Dietrich Bonhoeffer on Handout 2-A is from *Letters and Papers from Prison,* by Dietrich Bonhoeffer, translated from the German by R.H. Fuller (New York: Macmillan Publishing Company, 1963), pages 18–20. Copyright © 1971 by SCM Press Ltd. Reprinted with the permission of Scribner, an imprint of Simon & Schuster Adult Publishing Group and SCM Press Ltd.

The poem on Handout 2-B, "Created for Service," is by Cardinal John Henry Newman, and is taken from *Treasury of the Catholic Church: Two Thousand Years of Spiritual Writing,* compiled by Teresa de Bertodano (London: Darton, Longman and Todd, 1999), page 190. Copyright © 1999 by Teresa de Bertodano.

The text paraphrased on page 63 is from *How Good Do We Have to Be?: A New Understanding of Guilt and Forgiveness,* by Harold S. Kushner (Ringwood, Australia: Viking, 1996), pages 120, 121, and 123. Copyright © 1996 by Harold S. Kushner. All rights reserved.

The text on page 65 is taken from *The Powers That Be: Theology for a New Millenium* by Walter Wink (New York: Galilee Doubleday, 1998), page 48. Copyright © 1998 by Augsburg Fortress. All rights reserved.

The excerpt of "The Two Wolves" is paraphrased and found at *www .learntofeelgood.com/twowolves.atml*

The text on page 78 is quoted from chapter 9 of *Called to Covenant* by Clare vanBrandwijk (Winona, MN: Saint Mary's Press). Copyright © 2004 by Saint Mary's Press. All rights reserved.

The story on page 80 is quoted from *Matthew, Mark, Luke & You* by William J. O'Malley (Allen, TX: Thomas More, 1996), pages 50–51. Copyright © 1996 by William S. O'Malley. All rights reserved. Used with permission.

Handout 4-A is adapted from "For Every Woman" by Nancy R. Smith, in *Images of Women in Transition,* compiled by Janice Grana (Winona, MN: Saint Mary's Press, 1991), page 49. Copyright 1976 by The Upper Room, Nashville, Tennessee. Used with permission of Upper Room Books.

The excerpt at the beginning of Handout 4-B is from the English translation of the *Catechism of the Catholic Church* for use in the United States of America (CCC), numbers 2332, 2337, 2342, 2347, 2354, and 2362. Copyright © 1994 by the United States Catholic Conference, Inc.—Libreria Editrice Vaticana.

The text by The Sacred Congregation for Catholic Education on Handout 4-B is taken from *Educational Guidance in Human Love: Outlines for Sex Education* (Homebush, Australia: St. Paul Publications), pages 9–10 and 19–20.

The quote paraphrased from Plato on page 99 is taken from *The Holy Longing: The Search for a Christian Spirituality,* by Ronald Rolheiser (New York: Doubleday, 1999), page 1. Copyright © 1999 by Ronald Rolheiser. All rights reserved.

Prayer "A Blessing of Solitude" on page 103 is adapted from *Anam Cara* by John O'Donohue (London: Bantam Press, 1997), page 161. Copyright © 1997 by John O'Donohue. All rights reserved. Permission applied for.

"Prayer of an Unknown Confederate Soldier" on Handout 5-A is reprinted from *A Man's Guide to Prayer,* by Linus Mundy (New York: The Crossroad Publishing Company, 1998), pages 36–37. Copyright © 1998 by Linus Mundy. All rights reserved. Permission applied for.

Poem "God help us . . ." on Handout 5-A is adapted from *A Common Prayer* by Michael Leunig (North Blackburn, Australia: HarperCollins Dove, 1990). Copyright © 1990 by Michael Leunig. Used with permission.

Prayer "Blessed are you . . ." on Handout 5-A is adapted from *Prayers for the Domestic Church: A Handbook for Worship in the Home,* by Edward Hays (Easton, KS: Forest of Peace Books, Inc., 1979), page 59. Copyright © 1979 by Edward M. Hays. Used with permission.

Resource 5-A is reprinted from *It Was on Fire When I Lay Down on It* by Robert Fulghum (London: Grafton Books, 1989), pages 93–97. Copyright © 1988, 1989 by Robert Fulghum. Used with permission of Villard Books, a division of Random House, Inc.

The quote by e.e. cummings on Handout 5-B is adapted and taken from appearing in *The Ethiopian Tattoo Shop,* by Edward Hays (Leavenworth, KS: Forest of Peace Publishing, Inc., 1983), page 60. Copyright © 1983 by Edward M. Hays. Used with permission.

The poem "A Prayer to Own Your Beauty" by Macrina Wiederkehr on Handout 5-B is taken from *Seasons of Your Heart: Prayers and Reflections,* by Macrina Wiederkehr (New York: HarperCollinsPublishers, 1991), page 71. Copyright © 1991 by Macrina Wiederkehr. All rights reserved. Used with permission of HarperCollinsPublishers, Inc.

Poem on Handout 5-B by Thomas Merton is taken from *A Seven Day Journey with Thomas Merton,* by Esther de Waal (Ann Arbor, MI: Servant Publications, 1992), pages 37–38. Copyright by Esther de Waal. Permission applied for.

To view copyright terms and conditions for Internet materials cited here, log on to the home pages for referenced Web sites.

During this book's preparation, all citations, facts, figures, names, addresses, telephone numbers, Internet URLs, and other information cited within were verified for accuracy. The authors and Saint Mary's Press staff have made every attempt to reference current and valid sources, but we cannot guarantee the content of any source, and we are not responsible for any changes that may have occurred since our verification. If you find an error in, or have a question or concern about, any of the information or sources listed within, please contact Saint Mary's Press.